CW00506353

RISE
TOGETHER

A leaders' guide to the science
behind creating innovative, engaged
and resilient employees

DR SAM MATHER

Re think

First published in Great Britain in 2021
by Rethink Press (www.rethinkpress.com)

© Copyright Sam Mather

All rights reserved. No part of this publication may be reproduced, stored in or introduced into a retrieval system, or transmitted, in any form, or by any means (electronic, mechanical, photocopying, recording or otherwise) without the prior written permission of the publisher.

The right of Sam Mather to be identified as the author of this work has been asserted by her in accordance with the Copyright, Designs and Patents Act 1988.

This book is sold subject to the condition that it shall not, by way of trade or otherwise, be lent, resold, hired out, or otherwise circulated without the publisher's prior consent in any form of binding or cover other than that in which it is published and without a similar condition including this condition being imposed on the subsequent purchaser.

Cover image © Shutterstock | birulaut03

To my father, Ken Mather.

I miss you and think of you every day. You gave me what I needed to be where I am. I hope this would have made you proud.

d. September 2019

Contents

Introduction

The Covid-19 outbreak has provided us all with a tragic reminder of the environment in which organisations currently operate. Adopted from the US military over a decade ago, the term 'VUCA' – volatile, uncertain, complex and ambiguous – describes unpredictable environments. Driven by globalisation, economic and political instability, social and cultural shifts, and rapid technological change, today's VUCA working environment is synonymous with new and unexpected challenges.[1]

In developing the RISE principles, I conducted research into the resources that employees need to maximise their performance in today's workplace, and I gathered data from employees working in industries such as IT, Financial Services, Manufacturing,

Media, Construction and Education. This book explains the findings of my research and applies them to organisations and their leaders. There is also a parallel book aimed at helping individuals such as employees RISE in all areas of their lives.

You should read this book if:

- You recognise that if you need to send your employees to resilience training or employee referral programmes, it's too late – their resources have already been depleted and their resilience has failed. It is far better to prevent the need for such safety nets in the first place.

- You want your organisation's performance to RISE, and you are smart enough to know that this requires the performance of its people to RISE.

- You are looking for a well-researched, scientifically backed approach that is easy (and fun!) to read and that is applicable in the workplace.

Using simple metaphors, clear diagrams, questionnaires and step-by-step guides, this book will enable you and your leadership team to get the most from the people you work with. If you want your organisation to remain competitive and succeed in today's environments, this book is for you.

Why now? Lessons from a virus

The Covid-19 pandemic epitomised the VUCA environment. The world was facing an unprecedented challenge, and people, organisations and countries were dealing with 'unknown unknowns'.[2] We all faced problems that had not occurred to us before – problems that required novel solutions. To remain operational, let alone competitive, organisations needed to adapt quickly and innovatively to meet these new environmental demands.[3]

How did your organisation fare when Covid-19 hit?

Many firms shut down, some laying off staff. However, organisations that adapted quickly were able to manage and maintain production. Formula One manufacturers such as McLaren and Red Bull used their rapid prototype production skills to make ventilators. Fashion house Burberry began to produce protective surgical masks, and educational establishments found new ways to teach students via online media.

Of course, we hope there will never be another situation like the Covid-19 pandemic, but these days change is the norm in organisations.[4] The environments in which organisations operate are dynamic, fast moving and uncertain, and the consequence of such rapid and continuous change is increased ambiguity and uncertainty[5] for both organisations and their employees.[6]

This book will provide you with a neurological perspective on how having SOUND employees can help your organisation's performance RISE. By understanding the relationship between resources and the brain, this book will provide a template to enable your organisation to be **R**esilient and **I**nnovative, to **S**hift and **E**volve.

What are SOUND employees?

> **sound** (*adj*) **1.** not broken or damaged, healthy
> or in good condition. **2.** showing or based
> on good judgement. **3.** complete or detailed.
> **4.** able to be trusted because of having a lot of
> ability or knowledge. **5.** not harmful of wrong[7]

A 'SOUND' employee is 'resource-full'. They create, build and maintain the right cognitive, emotional and physical resources that they need and then deploy them in a way that is flexible, adaptable, innovative, smart, positive, self-aware, engaged and successful. A SOUND employee is able to do this in both good times and bad. This is because a SOUND employee is one who is able to:

- **S**ustain themselves and, in particular, their brain for maximum performance.

- **C**reate meaning and purpose in their life through the realisation of their **O**mnipurpose.

- Ensure positive cognitive resources through the application of a **U**seful **N**arrative.

- Be **D**iscerning about where they focus their attention to ensure sufficient cognitive resources for productive activities.

This may sound similar to resilience, defined as the process, or 'capacity for successful adaptation despite challenging or threatening circumstances',[8] which is considered to be a result of normal, basic human adaptation systems.[9] This normal adaptation system is generally effective – so effective, in fact, that our means of coping with stressors can kill us.

For years, we can deploy all of our resources to cope with stress, until the day we become seriously mentally or physically ill. The Machiavellian organisations may say, 'Well, we got a good twenty years out of him' but, in fact, they didn't. During the twenty years when the employee exhausted all of their resources in coping, that employee had reduced brain function. Employees with depleted resources are unable to process information fully, leading to negative attitudes,[10] cynicism,[11] emotional responses,[12] and an inability to adapt, change or be innovative.

Being resilient is merely doing the basics to make it from one day to the next. For an organisation, it means twenty years of an employee thinking inside the box, resisting change, being negative and lacking engagement. What a waste: a lose-lose scenario.

SOUND employees go beyond reactively cop-ing because they are resource-full. They achieve this state by knowing themselves: which resources deplete them and which replenish them. People who are SOUND monitor their resource levels, and they actively seek and develop the resources that they need when they need them. Having gained these resources, the SOUND employee chooses where to invest and deploy them. They use their resources to manage their environment, rather than the environment managing their resources.

SOUND employees are able to manage their thoughts and emotions, recognising that these can use up resources unnecessarily. In understanding that the brain can work with or against them, they manage it accordingly, creating clarity of thought and ratio-nal responses. A SOUND person has the resources – and desire – to learn, grow and become better every day. They enable themselves to RISE: be **R**esilient and **I**nnovative, **S**hift and **E**volve. Having an organ-isation full of SOUND employees will enable your organisation to RISE too.

The bad news is that implementing well-being pro-grammes alone may not change either your employ-ees or your organisation's performance. As this book will show, they may not help at all. But the good news is that research has shown there are ways to turn employees – including yours – into SOUND people.

PART ONE
THE THEORY

Before we look at the tools and techniques to create SOUND employees, it is worth spending some time looking at the mechanics of the brain. What it does, why and how you, as a leader, can influence not only your own brain but those of others. I often compare this to a car. My car gets me from a to b as long as I provide it with fuel and check the oil and tyres now and again. That's all I need (or frankly want) to know. Until I start to hear 'a funny noise' indicating that all is not well and things start to go wrong. The car's performance begins to falter. Its fuel efficiency drops. Despite gazing under the bonnet, I have no idea what to do, or how to improve the performance. So, I outsource this to a mechanic who sucks their teeth and slowly shakes their head, exclaiming that whatever the ailment is, it'll cost me.

And I can live with this when it comes to my car. But it's a different story with my brain. There are times when outsourcing the performance of our brain to a counsellor or therapist is beneficial. However, I would like to be able to address any performance issues before it gets that far. To do so I need to understand the mechanics of my brain, so I can tweak and amend its performance before 'it costs me'.

Therefore, the first section of the book introduces the brain and how it responds in today's organisations. By starting here, you will be able to lead in a way that ensures it doesn't 'cost' your organisation.

1
Balloons, Brains And Biology

The brain is the organ in the body that determines how we deploy our resources. This process may happen in the background – sometimes we are unaware of where our resources are being invested – so our starting point will be understanding how the human brain uses resources and why.

Think of psychological resources as inputs into our brains. The brain's 100 million neurons are constantly receiving input from both external and internal sources,[13] and we may not be aware of all the input as our brains are able to 'dull' attention paid to non-threatening, regular inputs. You may not be aware of the noise of a plane flying overhead, but if that plane exploded above you the sound would signal a potential threat and focus your attention. Similarly, we are receiving input from within, and often we are unaware of it unless it becomes a problem. We are not aware of how our shoes feel on our feet unless they begin to hurt. We will discuss specific psychological resources in later chapters; for now, consider them 'stuff that goes into your brain' – what you hear, see, touch, taste and smell, as well as thoughts and emotions.

In the context of organisations, providing employees with external job-related resources such as job security, rewards, feedback and supervisor support has been shown to be motivational, contributing to job satisfaction and protecting against burnout.[14] However, little has been written about the internal psychological resources that people need to succeed. Experts cite psychological resources ranging from 'authenticity' to 'wisdom' as leading to resilience,[15] and not all are easy to change or develop. But in this book we are looking for more than resilience – we are looking for employees to RISE.

RISE like a hot-air balloon

Despite the obvious jokes about 'air-heads', the hot-air balloon is a great analogy for the relationship between resources and our brains.

One operates a hot-air balloon by filling it with the right mix of resources (hot and/or cold air, or perhaps propane) so that it strengthens enough to stand upright and then to cut through the surrounding air pressure and rise.

Once in the air, the balloon's pilot constantly monitors the environment using all their senses. The pilot observes what is happening to the balloon, they watch the speed of the clouds and the type of cloud formation. They listen to the air being released from the canisters, the wind, and the creaking of the ropes that wrap around the balloon and the basket. Their sense of smell, and possibly also taste, is on alert for the distinctive metallic-chlorine smell of ozone, which can predict a storm. Most importantly, the pilot is tuning in to the rise and fall of the balloon, the strength of wind resistance and any changes in temperature. By evaluating the environment, the pilot can adjust the resource mix accordingly to ensure the balloon remains inflated, stable and afloat, letting its passengers safely reach new heights and gain new perspectives.

It is true that the hot-air balloon is fallible. It operates as a unit: a tear in one part of the balloon may not result in the balloon plunging to the ground but will certainly impact the efficiency of its performance as the resources leak unproductively into the atmosphere. The more tears, the less efficient it is and the more likely it will crash and burn. Steering a hot-air balloon is somewhat hit and miss: you have an idea of where you are going but the Atlantic jet stream may have other ideas. Adjusting the resource mix and the balloon's height may compensate for the jet stream; if not, the resources ensure you get back on the ground safely – wherever that may be. In fact, balloonists see this as part of the fun: you never know where you will end up!

Now, let's compare that with the human brain.

We are surrounded by information, some of which can create stress: work, family, neighbours, health, the economy, whether Newcastle United football team will be promoted next season. To function and 'rise above' these stressors, our brains need the right resources. Adding copious amounts of the wrong resources (alcohol, chocolate, binge watching Netflix) will not help, nor will an insufficient quantity of the right resources. Trying to inflate a hot-air balloon with a hairdryer – even the fancy £500 ones – just won't cut it. A brain that has the right mix of resources will let its owner think clearly, effectively process stimuli from the environment, make better decisions, adopt new perspectives and achieve new heights of success.

But how do we know what the right resources are? Like the hot-air balloon pilot, we use our senses of sight, sound and smell. But the most powerful way we receive information is through our feelings.

The primary purpose of the brain is to keep us alive. In this respect, little has changed since the evolution of *Homo erectus* 2 million years ago. The brain achieves this objective by differentiating danger from safety using a mechanism that we know as 'feelings'. Feelings are hormonal responses to the environment that tell us whether something is right or wrong, a threat or safe, something to avoid or approach. If we feel light-headed, nauseous and angry, we probably need food resources. If we have a headache, we may need water. These are, in the simplest terms, the body telling us we are lacking in a resource. Feelings are a complex area that we will explore throughout this book.

As with a hot-air balloon, the input of the right mix of resources into our brains will create SOUND employees, and, like the hot-air balloon, they will RISE: be resilient and innovative, shift their thinking and evolve. However, if one could achieve improved performance simply by stuffing an employee's head with resources, then this would be a short book. Three factors limit the resources we can give our brains: capacity, load and quality.

Capacity

For a hot-air balloon to carry four passengers, it requires 2.2 million litres of air. For comparison, an Olympic-sized swimming pool holds 2.5 million litres of water. We could try and squeeze in another million litres of air in an attempt to go higher and further for longer, but the balloon has a capacity limit; add more resources than it has capacity for, and it will explode. Like the balloon, there are only so many resources the brain can deal with at once. Too many resources, and the brain will metaphorically explode.

The brain is generally considered to have a finite resource capacity,[16] although this is debated. After all, if you think you have limited resource capacity then you probably will. Those who support the theory of unlimited resources tested resource depletion by measuring levels of willpower.[17] We all know that when we are tired, hungry or stressed our willpower leaves us and we indulge in cake/coffee/beer (choose your poison) because our sleep, glucose and cognitive resources are low. Studies found that participants who believed that their resources were limited were more likely to lose willpower, suggesting that resource depletion may be a result of believing that resources are finite. But what the study does not reveal is whether the belief that one has limited resources was related to the number of psychological resources participants had at the time. Perhaps a limited-resource mindset is itself a result of low resource levels. Furthermore, those with an unlimited-resource mindset may feel fatigue and experience ego depletion but either don't notice or don't react to it, while those who have a limited-resource mindset respond to ego depletion and choose to preserve their energies.[18]

Until there is a definitive answer to the question of resource limits, it is safer to assume that we have a limited resource capacity. This makes our resources precious, things to carefully cultivate and to use wisely. The SOUND employee knows that if something is limited, it is much more valuable, as we saw with toilet roll during the Covid-19 outbreak.

Load

Whether you view resource capacity as limited or unlimited, there is general agreement that facing excessive demands deplete resources.[19] Resilience is having enough resources to meet demand, and when you feel the demands on you are greater than what your resources can handle, then your resilience, or ability to cope, reduces. Imagine a tear in the hot-air balloon. Each tear represents a stressor through which your resources escape. As the balloon incurs more tears, or stressors, it will begin to sink.

Sometimes the overload process is slow, with small tears appearing over time. We have all been there, experiencing stress gradually mounting. A colleague resigns, leaving you with double the work. Your kitchen extension is two months behind schedule, due to the discovery of a rare toad living in your garden, leaving you with a camping stove for an oven and a bucket for a sink. Meanwhile you are worried about child number one, who suddenly spends all his time sitting in his bedroom listening to Pink Floyd/ The Smiths/Billie Eilish (select generation-relevant reference). The final straw was the police calling having found your mother wandering around the park in her dressing gown looking for Harrison Ford. Lots of little tears in your balloon, which individually would be manageable but together result in a significant loss of resources.

Sometimes the tear is a huge, unexpected rip that causes a rapid loss of altitude. A big event, such as a bereavement, job loss or illness, enters your life without warning, and all your resources are suddenly consumed by this event, diminishing your ability to deal with other aspects of life.

The technical term for this is 'allostatic load'.[20] 'Allostasis' is the collective term for the brain's adaptation processes that help manage our resources so that we maintain equilibrium. When we have to activate resources too often to cope with stressors, the consequence is allostatic load: wear and tear on our resources. This is because, when under stress, we release hormones such as cortisol and adrenaline. When we repeatedly deploy these hormones (lots of little tears in the balloon), or deploy them in large amounts (a huge rip), we deprioritise the areas of the brain that control smart thinking and learning.[21] Since cortisol and adrenaline 'eat up' cognitive resources, allostatic load (excessive demand) depletes resources.[22]

Sadly, we don't walk round with indicators of our current resource levels, so when someone lashes out at you for what you consider 'no apparent reason', the reality is that dealing with you required one more resource than they had. The demand on them exceeded their capacity.

What, then, is the resource capacity of a human brain, and what is the minimum number of resources with which we can effectively operate? It depends. For our hot-air balloon, the amount of hot air or propane needed to create and maintain altitude will depend on several factors. The warmer the outside temperature, the more propane or hot air we need. If the balloon is only carrying two passengers rather than ten, we'll need fewer resources. If the balloon already has a few small tears in it, we'll need more air/propane than if there were no tears. Similarly, how you cope with stressors depends on your experience, what else is happening in your environment, your personality and even how your parents dealt with stressors.

The process of allostasis (maintaining equilibrium) is a physiological one involving hormones that control the nervous system, the metabolic system, the gut, the kidneys and the immune system,[23] so your levels of health and fitness can also impact how efficiently you deploy resources to manage stressors.[24] Load is complicated and varies from person to person, day to day. But the SOUND employee is self-aware enough to know their load limit and manage their resources accordingly.

Quality

Now we know that resources are valuable due to their limited quantity, we need to consider which resources we keep and which we lose. Resources are inputs into our brain, but not all resources are created equally; some add to our capacity and others will deplete our resources, like adding a fox into a henhouse. Since adding any old resource into someone's head will not automatically make them SOUND, quality is an issue.

How do you know which resources to let in? Your brain will send you messages as to which resources to avoid and which to approach – you just need to listen for them. The messages are better known as feelings.

When self-isolating during Covid-19, what made you feel negative and depressed and what improved your mood? Watching horror movies such as *Outbreak, Contagion* or *I am Legend* might have led to an increase in panic, while watching endless videos of cats on skateboards might have brought you inexplicable joy. The feelings these experiences generated were messages as to whether these inputs were beneficial or not: whether we should approach or avoid the stimuli.

In the context of work, your boss may praise you. That's an input that creates positive 'approach' feelings. Praise and reward are examples of positive resources; they help you RISE. By contrast, being shouted at in front of your colleagues will generate negative 'avoid' feelings; although it's also an input to the brain, it depletes your resources as you have to deploy a whole suite of them to prevent you crying, resigning, shouting back or running away.

Often resources themselves are neither positive nor negative – it is how they are delivered and/or in what context. Getting feedback can be a positive experience in which you learn about yourself, enabling you to RISE. Alternatively, poorly communicated feedback dripping with blame may generate negative feelings, decreasing your ability to RISE. Taking in one negative resource in a sea of positive resources is unlikely to make a significant impact, just as farting into a hot-air balloon (given the 2.2 million litres of much fresher air in there) is unlikely to impact performance. However, if the balloon contained more methane than fresh air, it is likely to lose altitude – and require a can of air freshener!

Good feelings, of course, do not always equal quality resources. Drugs, alcohol, smoking, chocolate, cake, spending sprees and revenge all generate good feelings… initially. The positive feelings generated usually wear off quickly. In small doses, these are fine provided they are not the only positive resources you input. Similarly, quality resources do not always generate good feelings, at first. Running, maths exams and childbirth are tough in the short term but increase resources in the long term. In the case of childbirth, it might be very long term.

There is also the subjective element of quality. Hobfoll defines resources as that which is 'valued by the individual'.[25] What one person values, another may not: some people may see a day spent watching cricket as time well spent, increasing their resources. Not for me, I'm afraid. Spending the day sleeping would be equally, if not more, beneficial for me – and as about as exciting.

Ensuring a plentiful supply of resources is a dark art, unique to each individual. While an exact formula will vary from person to person, the overarching principle is: the more positive resources a person has, the greater their ability to cope and manage stressors, and the greater the ability to RISE.[26]

Resources > Stressors = RISE

Key learnings from this chapter

- Resources are limited, which makes them valuable. Choose your resources wisely.

- There are two types of brain resources: positive ones make us feel good which is the brain telling us to "approach" or move toward the resource and negative ones which is the brain telling us to "avoid" that resource.

- For the brain to perform well, it needs more positive resources than negative resources.

2
Resources To RISE

L ike our well-filled hot-air balloon, we want our
employees – and our organisation – to RISE, reaching stratospheric levels of performance. This chapter explains why we need resources to achieve this
and what we mean by RISE. The brain is constantly
evaluating the environment, forming attitudes and
beliefs as to whether a situation is safe to approach
or whether to avoid it, and the brain conveys these
attitudes and beliefs to us through feelings and
emotions.

Our initial responses to everything are emotional,
and this is because emotional processing is a faster
process – eight times faster – than thinking logically.
Emotional processing needs to be so fast because this

is what helped us survive in the past. We needed to instantly ascertain whether that big kitty with the long teeth was to be approached or avoided. If we had relied on logic to consider our options, perform a risk analysis and create a project plan for the way forward, we would have had first-hand experience with those long teeth.

We will address how we deal with and respond to emotion in Part Two; for now, just recognise that everyone's first response is always emotional. Whether it's a head-office announcement, an employee's feedback, the decision to change the IT system or to implement a cashless canteen, or even changing the contents of the vending machine, emotions dictate the first response. None of these events are good or bad in themselves; they just are. It is your emotional response that will evaluate the event (not always correctly) as good (approach) or bad (avoid). The brain treats emotion as a source of information.[27]

Let's say a decision has been made to remove allocated parking spots in the office car park. Each employee has evaluated the information and formed an attitude towards it. Employee A responds angrily to this new parking arrangement. They are losing their allocated space and see it as both a personal slight on their status and as political correctness gone mad.

Employee A's brain has used emotion as information. Their negative emotional response has resulted in a negative resource. This type of information processing is termed 'peripheral processing'.[28] Emotionally driven, it requires few resources because it relies on past information and experience, so we don't have to process, evaluate or think too much.[29] One of the reasons we are greater risk takers when we are younger is that we have less knowledge or experience to inform our decisions. When I consider the gap year I spent throwing myself out of airplanes and off bridges tied to a piece of elastic, I wonder what possessed me. Happily for me at the time, what I didn't possess was any knowledge or experience about how either activity could go wrong.

Luckily, if we have sufficient resources, we can also apply some conscious thought to situations when appropriate. Employee B also had an immediate negative emotional response to the change in parking arrangements and wonders if sometimes the organisation makes changes for change's sake. However, Employee B has since thought about it and is now feeling more positive. They can see it is probably fairer and, after all, more people are working from home now.

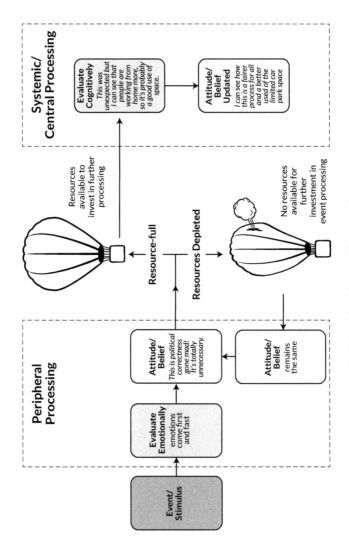

Peripheral and central processing

Employee B's additional thinking time generates a positive input into her brain and therefore adds to her resource level. Referred to as systemic or central processing, this requires investing some resources into cognitive processing and reflection.[30] Employee A's instant, emotional reaction to the new parking system was negative. However, if Employee A applies some thought, they may realise that this was not a policy designed to personally annoy them and that it's probably a more efficient use of limited parking spaces. This thought process mediates the initial emotion (anger)[31] and the negative resource becomes at least neutral, if not positive.

This cognitive processing and reflection is only possible if Employee A has the resources available to invest in further thinking beyond her emotional response. Research has shown that where resources are lacking, evaluations of the environment and events remain emotional.[32]

The output of evaluative processes are attitudes and beliefs. We are more likely to create positive attitudes when resources are plentiful because plentiful resources enable investment in logical thinking; otherwise, we rely only on our 'first and fast' emotional responses. It is this process that can create bias and prejudice. I have yet to determine what event or stimulus created my prejudice against men wearing soccer shirts (outside of a soccer match), but in being aware of the attitude I can invest resources in mitigating this illogical bias. I still *feel* the emotion, but I have the resources to manage it and tell myself to think differently. Eventually, my neurons will be reprogrammed when seeing a man in a soccer shirt from thinking, 'There's a man looking for a fight' to thinking, 'There's a man who enjoys watching sport and is proud of his team'.

In organisations, being able to apply systemic or central processing to the environment, organisation or events is key to being able to RISE. Choosing to evaluate organisational and leadership initiatives positively (or reframe them, if required) adds to your resources and helps create resilience. Employees with fewer resources will be less able to see events as positive, thereby decreasing their resources and their resilience.

R is for resilience

The definition of resilience is hard to pin down.[33] Most definitions of resilience refer to maintaining equilibrium or returning to pre-adversity functioning after a challenge.[34] Resilience is the result of our normal adaptation systems – the process of allostasis.[35] It's maintaining your resources to allow you to manage life: keeping the balloon afloat.

Some definitions broaden the idea of resilience, believing it's not only about maintaining equilibrium but also includes the process of bouncing back from adversity.[36] In other words, re-floating the balloon after events have caused it to sink to the ground.

There are some that go even further, asserting that resilience is not just about surviving adversity and bouncing back but also about thriving, learning and growing as a result of the adversity.[37] There is research both for[38] and against this thinking.[39]

There are a couple of issues with the latter conception of resilience. Firstly, what is meant by thriving and growth? Studies differ in their measurement: some include behaviours such as stopping drinking,[40] adopting deeper religious beliefs,[41] not taking life for granted,[42] and psychological changes such as having a sense of personal strength and increased spirituality.[43] Furthermore, if growth was an inherent part of resilience, every person who exercised resilience would grow from their challenging experience, which sadly is not always the case.[44] In an eighteen-year study of resilience in disadvantaged children, Egeland, Carlson and Sroufe found that adverse situations had a cumulative negative effect on competency rather than providing opportunities for growth beyond equilibrium.[45] The few who successfully 'bounced back' achieved what society would consider 'normal functioning'. Given the background of the participants, was this evidence of growth or merely reaching an acceptable level of equilibrium and functioning? It's also worth noting that if bouncing back is required, then the deployment of resources has already failed. Had the individual been able to maintain resilience, they would have nothing from which to bounce back in the first place.

Where the confusion lies is in combining two different motivational mechanisms and labelling them both 'resilience'. The first is our defensive motivational system: the drive to protect ourselves from harm, whether physical, emotional or financial. Often triggered by an emotional event, the defensive motivational system deploys resources to help us maintain equilibrium.[46] Using our hot-air balloon analogy, we are floating along, adequate resources enabling us to maintain altitude and head in the right direction, when along comes an unexpected gust of wind that unsteadies the balloon, which loses height and changes direction. The pilot will use all the resources at their disposal to return the balloon to its original position, but what if there are no more resources? The air tanks are empty, the pilot has run out of ideas and the balloon has insufficient resources to counteract the demands of the weather; thus, the balloon heads towards earth. At this stage, the motivation for resource deployment is defensive: preventing harm in the form of a sudden and rapid impact with the ground. During this time, emotions are probably running high, and if these emotions are negative (most likely, in the face of impending doom), research has shown that the ability to use systemic or central processing to apply reasoned and logical thinking is inhibited.[47] Whether the balloon actually hits the ground will depend on something changing: finding more resources or the weather improving.

Now, imagine implementing a new balloon inflation system during this time. It's quite different from the current method and requires learning a new process, so the chances of this new system being successful are slim. Balloon resources are depleted, and any remaining resources we have are being spent on preventing an impending collision. Our defensive motivational system is using what few resources we have to do exactly that: defend.

Growth comes from a different type of motivation: the appetite motivational system. Thriving and growing requires us to learn new things, to reflect and to create new neuronal connections; which is more likely to occur when there is a plentiful supply of resources and when we feel safe.[48] When we have the time and the resources to move from the quick, instinctive emotional responses of our defensive motivational system to the relative calm of the considered thoughts of our central processing system we are more likely to have an appetite for learning.

Not everyone grows and learns from adversity; some people merely return to previous levels of equilibrium. There are many reasons for this, which we will discuss in Chapter 3, but this is a choice and it leads to a 'return vs learn' decision. At this point, do you

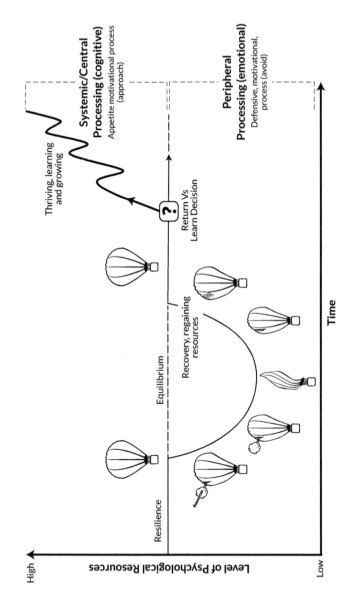

Defensive and appetite motivational processes

breathe a sigh of relief and continue along your merry way, or do you take time to reflect and learn from the process?

Consider the 'return vs learn' choice in the context of change. We expect employees to learn, grow, innovate, and be flexible, adaptable, positive and change agents; however, their resources are probably being deployed in coping with the uncertainty often associated with change (defensive motivational system). There are no spare resources for further development and growth.

After examining the defensive and appetite motivational processes, it seems resilience, recovery and growth are separate processes.[49] Resilience is the ability to continually deploy resources to maintain equilibrium. Recovery is the process of replenishing your resources to return to equilibrium, and it is only at the recovery point that you will have resources available to learn and grow. What researchers do agree on is that having enough of the right psychological resources enables resilience.[50]

SOUND employees are resilient because they know how to maintain the resources that they have or create new ones if needed. If there is a 'dip' in their resilience, they are able to recover from it more quickly than an employee who is not SOUND. In being resilient, they also have sufficient resources for initiative.

I is for initiative

Initiative, in the context of a person (rather than the latest company rollout plan), is the capacity to think independently, be inventive, cope with difficult or unusual problems, and be brave or confident in the face of a challenge. Organisations are usually looking for at least one of these qualities in their employees. The new and unexpected challenges – 'unknown unknowns'[51] prevalent in today's workplaces – are often ill-defined.[52] Simply using past knowledge or experience is no longer sufficient to solve such problems,[53] so companies need employees who can deal with novel problems and be bold in developing innovative ways to solve them. SOUND employees are able to do all this because they are resource-full. They have the resources to invest in the smart thinking needed for initiative.

If we are investing our resources in maintaining equilibrium, or we're trying to replenish our resources, we do not have the resource capacity to invest in smart and creative thinking. This is not only due to emotions as described above but also the physiological consequences of negative emotions in particular.

Think about a situation such as presenting to a large audience or having to fire an employee. Emotions always come first, and emotions are the physical effects of hormones. These effects might include feeling sick, needing to pee often, a racing heart and sweating. Even thinking about a stressful situation may cause emotional responses, although probably to a lesser degree than being faced with them.

These physiological responses are the consequences of the hormones cortisol and adrenaline – the 'fight or flight' hormones that keep you safe. They are not 'bad' hormones as they enabled you to respond speedily to our large-toothed feline friend in the previous section. These hormones enable speedy (and thus lifesaving) responses by strengthening the neuronal connections between memory retrieval (hippocampus) and the smart part of your brain (prefrontal cortex), enabling you to respond based on experience or by making a plan.

This is a clever and effective survival mechanism, but it only works to a point. When you become too stressed (ie, you do not feel you have sufficient resources to manage), your cortisol and adrenaline increase even further. This disables the link between the prefrontal cortex and the hippocampus, and you can no longer remember things or come up with a plan. These hormones go so far as to shut off some of your cognitive resources – the ones you don't need for fight or flight – proving that while some stress can help thinking, too much stress reduces it.

In our balloon scenario, when the bad weather hits, the pilot can manage the balloon by adjusting resources. When the bad weather becomes a force 10 storm, they dispense any resource not needed to keep that balloon in the air: picnic baskets, cameras, binoculars and even bottles of champagne all go overboard. They are not key resources to keeping afloat. No, not even the champagne.

The same happens to individuals. When cortisol and adrenaline are coursing through your veins, your brain deprioritises the resource that is not needed to maintain equilibrium. These hormones may disrupt your digestive process (so you might feel sick). The increase in adrenaline may make you pee often because the adrenal glands sit above the kidneys. Your heart rate may increase, getting you ready to run or fight, which in turn increases your temperature (sweating). Your peripheral vision narrows[54] and your hearing also reduces,[55] forcing you to focus on only the information needed to survive. This process helps us deploy our limited resources, and, with fewer resources and choices to deal with, our responses are quicker.

The cost of this quicker response and survival mechanism is that resources in the 'smart' part of your brain are metaphorically thrown out of the basket, along with the champagne. Cortisol and adrenaline shut down cognitive resources not needed to survive, such as knowledge of Greek mythology, your ability to cook a great chicken tikka masala and your ability to solve quadratic equations. Whether the threat is a sabre-toothed tiger, an upcoming presentation or a meeting to fire an employee, stress hormones can compromise the effectiveness of the brain's executive and cognitive function – in other words, the smart bit.[56]

When an employee is operating in survival mode, their reduced resources result in a narrowed view since they don't have the resources to process anything beyond their emotions and the here and now. Actions and responses will be quick but emotionally driven. It's not that they aren't capable of thought and consideration; rather, at that point in time, they don't have access to the cognitive resources needed to be smart or show initiative.

For employees to show initiative, then, they should operate in a state that enables smart thinking. Dopamine is an essential neurotransmitter which enables the neurons in parts of the brain responsible for learning, recalling memories and thinking creatively to work efficiently. When cortisol is high, dopamine is low; and when dopamine is high, cortisol is low.[57] The prefrontal cortex of the brain (the smart bit) manages dopamine and cortisol levels, as long as it has adequate resources; so, to maintain our dopamine when we feel under threat, we need resources.

Having sufficient resources to think beyond the initial emotional responses to more thought-through responses allows further processing. As a result, you're able to see the bigger picture beyond the here and now.[58] Those with sufficient resources are able to plan for the future. Operating in the appetite motivational system, they can create goals and, importantly, create strategies to reach these goals.

Having plentiful resources enables activation of the smart part of our brain. It even allows us to invest resources into creative and innovative ideas, knowing that the investment may not pay off. Not all creative ideas work, after all. One creative individual thought of (and manufactured) a boiled egg squarer, which makes your hard-boiled eggs square. Including the yolk. It never took off (can't think why), but it shows that at some point someone had enough surplus resources to invest in creating something new. OK, this one wasn't particularly successful, but it only takes one working idea...

In order for our employees to display initiative, they need plentiful resources to reduce cortisol and increase dopamine, enabling thinking using the smart part of the brain rather than just emotional responses. Dopamine is also associated with a positive mood, which has been shown to enable big-picture thinking,[59] letting employees think ahead, be creative and have the courage to try something new.

S is for shifting

Up to this point we have seen that there are two approaches to interpreting the world: emotional and cognitive. These approaches are also known as 'heart vs head', 'System 1 and System 2' or 'fast and slow thinking'. Both approaches have their pros and cons, and it is the tension between them that often makes decisions difficult, particularly in organisations. Making redundancies or restructures, or even just asking someone to do something you know they won't enjoy is always tough. This is because, although our head tells us the task needs to be done, our heart feels heavy knowing it may cause distress. As painful as this tension can be, we need both the head and the heart. Kaplan and Norton operationalised this duality for organisations with their Balanced Scorecard, which contains both 'head based' measures – Financial and Processes – and 'heart based' ones – Customer and Learning & Growth (which usually incorporates staff development).[60]

Traditionally, organisations measured their performance with financial data alone; however, this can result in nefarious business practices at worst, as profit becomes the key driver, or unwise decisions at best. The key being able to shift between perspectives to ensure you are evaluating all the information: the strategic and the operational, the people and the process, the immediate and the long term. Table 1 offers examples of perspective shifts.

Table 1: Perspective shifts

Low level of resources: emotional responses	High level of resources: emotional & cognitive responses
Narrow focus: what's in it for me?	AND big picture: what's in it for others?
The here and now	AND the future
Exploit	AND explore

A key advantage in these VUCA times – one crucial to coping with change – is the ability to shift between the 'exploit' and 'explore' perspectives. Deciding whether to exploit existing resources or to explore new ones is a survival decision. Consider the great Serengeti migration of wildebeest: from January to March, the herd are to be found in the south of the Serengeti feeding on the short grass and drinking from waterholes that were replenished during the rains of December. The herd is exploiting the favourable environment to feed and calve. However, by March the grass is eroded, the watering holes drying up. The herd could stay where they are, eking out an existence by exploiting the little remaining grass and water, but there is a risk here. There may not be enough food or water to go around and herd members may die of starvation. The herd decides to move, exploring alternative food sources, although this, too, is risky. They may not find a new grassy nirvana, and herd members may (and do) die during such treacherous journeys, but they know that staying where they are will lead to certain starvation.

Exploring is scary. It's the unknown. There might be nothing out there, or there is something but you don't know how to deal with it. It is safer to stay where you are, exploiting what you have, in an environment you are familiar with.

Spencer Johnson's book *Who Moved My Cheese?* explains this survival decisions pattern in the context of organisational change in an easy-to-read way.[61] In days gone by, organisations were filled with people who did the same job, in the same place with the same people for many years – sometimes their whole working lives. It was safe. The employee knew what they were doing; risk was minimal. Why on earth would they risk exploring something new?

To answer this question, let's consider the example of changing jobs and workplaces. If you've ever taken on a new job in a new company, what were your reasons for deciding to stop exploiting what you knew and explore something different? Often, there is more than one reason, but your motivations will be either to avoid (I hate my boss and need to get away from them) or approach (I want to get experience in a new sector).

If someone's motivations are avoid driven, they will only explore the new (change) when the pain of the current situation is greater than the fear of the unknown. This is known as the stick approach – if you do not change, you will be punished – and it is the standard approach to change management in organisations. Employees must comply or suffer. The drive to 'avoid' originates from the part of the brain responsible for fear: the amygdala. Fear creates stress, and too much stress can reduce our smart thinking.

If, on the other hand, the drive to explore is approach motivated – the carrot approach – the individual themselves will drive the change. The drive to 'approach' comes from the part of the brain that is reward focused and stimulates dopamine (which you will remember is important for learning and motivation).

In today's organisations, change and its increasing pace have become the norm.[62] The consequence of such rapid and continuous change is that organisations are less predictable and stable, resulting in increased ambiguity and uncertainty.[63] It's all scary, now. We are expected to be able to cleverly exploit what we have available, while also exploring innovative ways to do things. Despite this there are still some people who are resistant to change. If they were a wildebeest, they would rather manage on the meagre pickings of a dry savannah than risk leaving what they know for the potential of new feeding grounds. These are the employees who have low resource levels, and leaders can become exasperated at their passive aggressive attempts to avoid adopting new processes or technologies.

As the sections above explained, when resources are low our focus narrows to the immediate and the personal. In the context of the employee, this usually manifests as emotional responses concerned with the self: 'What does this mean for me and my job?' Exploring something new may mean learning and doing something different, and they don't have the resources for that as they are investing them in survival. Furthermore, the pressure to change is causing more tears in their balloon, resulting in the loss of more resources as they are pushed more into survival mode and away from smart thinking. The downward spiral continues, often resulting in stress-related mental health issues for the employee.

Employees who are resource-full are able to move beyond the immediate 'What does that mean for me?' emotional response to a broader view, enabling them to also consider their team, the organisation, the customer or the strategy. They can shift from explore to exploit, seeing both the now and the future. When finding solutions, they are able to exploit the known and existing solutions and to explore untried innovation options, combining the best of both if needed. When making decisions, they can evaluate what is best for the organisation and the employees, now and in the future. They are able to flex and broaden their thinking and responses, resulting in better decision making and better problem solving, making them a better employee.

A further benefit of being willing to explore is the ability to grow and learn. Those who sit happily in the same job for ten years have one year's experience repeated ten times over, rather than ten years' cumulative experience. Evolving requires exploring.

E is for evolving

Being able to shift thinking is key to evolving. After all, if the wildebeests had decided not to take the explore option, they would have died out by now. As Darwin noted, it is those who are able to evolve that survive. And just as organisations need to evolve to survive, so do the employees within them.

Irrespective of organisational demands, the SOUND employee evolves as a person, by choice. They see themselves as a work in progress, learning and growing with each passing year. They evolve not just because an organisation requires them to, but because they want to. They are exploring who they are, unafraid of new experiences and alternative viewpoints. Returning to equilibrium is not an option for them; at the point of the 'return or learn' decision, they choose to learn and grow from adversity.

Evolving is not surface-level learning based on your defence motivation system; it is deeper self-learning from your appetite motivation system. Let's say you realise you have made an error in performing a task for your boss. You can fix it, but it will take time – time you don't have given your to-do list. Rather than cover up the error, you decide to come clean with your boss and tell them what has happened, hoping they will understand when you don't complete the other things on your to-do list. Your boss instead responds angrily and demands that you fix the error, but without compromising any of the other things on your to-do list.

What's the learning here?

We all respond emotionally at first, showing surface-level learning using peripheral processing, coming from a defensive motivation. Your 'avoid' learnings may be that your boss hates bad news or is emotionally volatile and that you should 'never admit your mistakes – next time, cover them up'. You return to the task and carry on as before, but your resources are now deployed in ensuring you cover your tracks.

If you are resource-full, on the other hand, you can invest your resources in gaining deeper learnings using your appetite motivation (approach/toward). To enable evolutionary learning, consider asking yourself:

- Why did I make that mistake? What do I need to do differently in future?

- How might I have approached my boss differently to get a different response?

In this example, it's true your boss could have responded differently, but we are all human and your boss may have been having a bad day. After they have calmed down, they may decide to sit with you to ask the questions that create deeper learning. Or not. We will discuss the role of leaders in Part Two, but a SOUND employee will ask themselves these types of questions anyway because they prompt learning through self-exploration and understanding. This adds to their resources.

Evolving does not create immunity from resource loss. If we zoom in on the 'thriving, learning and growing' line in our processes model earlier in the chapter, we can see that although the trend is upward, there are moments when our resources deplete because learning about ourselves can be challenging.

For many years, I worked in a financial services company managing a team of around thirty people. I threw myself into my job – at my desk by 7am, not leaving until after 6pm. Our department was achieving great success: measures were in place and customers were happy. If only the team was a bit more enthusiastic. After about six months, I received some feedback from HR that my team was not happy. How could this be? We had transformed and we were successful; surely I was an amazing boss. Apparently not.

Although it was never explicitly stated, the team felt that they were expected to work the same long hours I did, my behaviour implicitly communicating this. I was the first in and the last out. As far as the team were concerned, I was always at work and that was the standard I set – a standard they felt they were failing to meet. If you think you are failing, then your resources will deplete. I had a team with low resources for this reason, and I'd been wondering why they weren't enthusiastic about the changes in the department.

I was shocked. It was never my intention to make my team feel like failures! I began unpicking my actions, recognising how my behaviour as a leader set the 'rules', intentionally or otherwise. This led to many soul-searching questions about why I behave the way I do, my drivers and who I was. There were some uncomfortable answers, which tested my resilience, and I questioned myself as a leader. Because of this learning, I evolved as a person and a leader and continued to thrive and grow. Evolutionary learning consumes resources, which means you can only learn if you have the resources available to invest in the quest for learning.

Learning is a biological process in the brain. It involves the creation of neurons that connect together. It is hugely complex and there is still much to learn about the brain, but for the sake of understanding the process of learning, here is a simplified description.

Imagine a child who has developed a phobia of dogs after being bitten by one. This phobia is due to neuronal connections: a memory was created when a neuron connected 'dog' with 'bite'. Without intervention, every time the child sees a dog the neuron between 'dog' and 'bite' gets stronger, reinforcing the association. To protect against any future pain from dog bites, the brain creates an emotional response to send a message of 'avoid'. In this case, the emotion is fear. This is a learned response.

The stimulus itself is neither good or bad, neither positive or negative; it is how we interpret it and what we associate it with that creates this judgement. This relates to our learned responses. For example, an ex-boyfriend of mine loved camping. In tents. On the ground. He grew up in a hot country where summers were guaranteed and camping trips were a chance to enjoy nature at its best: the sun, the sea and fun fun fun. Meanwhile, in the UK, my experience of summer camping was fighting the wind to put up (and keep up) the tent, only to sit in it for a week watching nature at its worst. I abandoned the holiday when I woke up unable to move as my four-season sleeping bag had absorbed half the river, which had burst its banks overnight. Hell, hell, hell.

Learning is about creating new neurons with new connections. Sometimes we have to 'unlearn' as well – if we change a process or a system at work, we need to unlearn the old process and learn the new one.

This means 'rewiring' the neuron. The more we use the new neuron, the stronger the connection gets; the less we use a neuron, the weaker it gets. This explains why if you don't practise and continually use a neuronal connection, it will fade.

For the dog phobia, new learning needs to take place to change the response to the 'dog' stimulus.

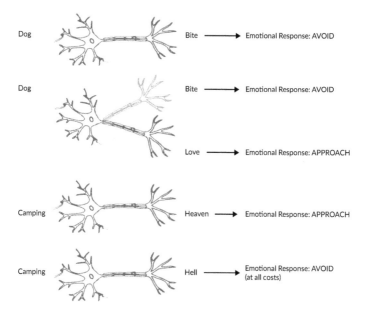

Neuronal connections between a stimulus and two outcomes

I am not doing this rewiring exercise with camping. It's *never* going to happen, which just goes to show that you can only rewire a neuron if there is a willingness to make the effort. And it is an effort. Just think of when you have tried to change the way you do something: give up smoking, stop using the word 'but', start exercising more. It's effort-full, and when we are low on resources the effort may be too great because we need our resources to survive, not improve.

The key to strengthening the efficiency of neurons is dopamine, the neurotransmitter that depletes with cortisol. To strengthen new neurons that come with learning, you need dopamine. And for dopamine to be high, you need to be resource-full. In the context of organisations, this is particularly relevant for change. If you are asking people to perform differently, learn new things and evolve, they need lots of dopamine, and they won't have it if their resources are low and they are in survival mode.

At this point in the book, I am hoping you are convinced of the need for SOUND employees who can RISE and enable your organisation to RISE along with them. The question you may be asking now is, 'OK, so how do I get resource-full employees?' Well, I am glad you asked because the answer's in the next section!

QUESTIONS FOR YOUR ORGANISATION

- How is 'emotion' viewed within your organisation? Why?
- What mechanisms are in place to encourage a 'learn' versus a 'return' decision?
- How are employees encouraged to manage and

increase their cognitive resources?

- How are employees encouraged to explore and evolve?

Key learnings from this chapter

🎈 The brain is constantly scanning the environment to determine if we should approach or avoid the stimuli.

🎈 Emotional processing (peripheral) comes first and fast.

🎈 Central processing requires cognitive resources.

🎈 Having sufficient cognitive resources will enable employees to be resilient, show initiative, shift perspectives and move towards evolving.

🎈 Learning is the process of neurons in the brain making connections. And the good news is they can be rewired.

3
The Rock Of Fear

The science has convinced you that SOUND employees will benefit your organisation, but where do we find them? Where is the switch to make employees SOUND? There must be a switch, because organisations recruit positive, enthusiastic, capable and SOUND employees all the time but two years later they are negative, disillusioned and indifferent. Did someone switch the SOUND off?

The employee certainly has a part to play, and although in my other book, *RISE*, written for individuals, I explore this idea in more depth, Chapter 8 in this book provides a summary of the employee's role in becoming SOUND. However, the nature of an organisation can unwittingly deplete an employee's resources quicker than the employee can replenish them, and the greatest consumer of resources is fear.

Fear is not a bad thing per se. It is a valuable warning signal, albeit a powerful one, but it needs to be to ensure our survival. Imagine if we could turn off our fear. I am not sure I would last a day, and I certainly would not have made it through my gap year. However, fear triggers our defensive mechanisms: cortisol, 'avoid' responses and emotional processing. It narrows our focus, prioritising only the resources we need to survive. Fear can also defy logic, as my fear of cruise ships attests (I've never even been on a cruise ship!).

Imagine I lay a plank of wood 3 metres long and half a metre wide on the ground (that's about 10ft by 1.5ft in old money). If I bet you your tipple of choice that you couldn't walk along it, you would likely accept the bet and win the drink. No problem.

Now, if I were to place the same plank between the roofs of two ten-storey buildings, would you still take the bet? You know you can walk the plank, so logically you can take on the bet, but fear has kicked in. Maybe if I offered you a larger incentive you'd take the bet; however, the incentive would vary for different people. It would depend on the tension between your defensive motivation (the value of protecting what you have, namely your life) and your appetite motivation (the value of what you may gain).

Going back to our balloon metaphor, we all drag our fears with us like a rock. The Rock of Fear (in my head this is said in a booming, ominous voice, maybe with a spooky soundtrack) is the weight of our fears we carry with us. This is why you can't run away from your fears; whichever direction the balloon of life takes you, your fears are right there with you. So, for our balloon to RISE we need sufficient resources to elevate the balloon *and* the Rock of Fear. If your fear is boulder sized, you will need a large number of resources to maintain equilibrium and RISE, and you'll find this difficult and exhausting. A small tear in the balloon will have a greater effect on your equilibrium than it would for someone with only a pebble of fear. A pebble of fear will also weigh you down but won't consume as many resources; thus, replenishment of resources will be easier, enabling a quicker return to equilibrium.

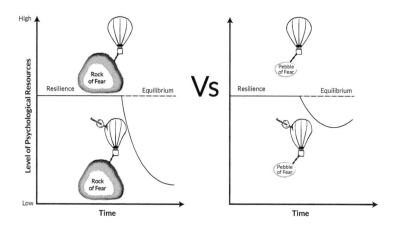

The effect of the Rock of Fear on resilience

There are many names for fear that manifest in behaviour. Anger is a common one. Anger is the only emotion that is both approach and avoid. Combined with sufficient resources, the appetite motivational system can use anger constructively to change things for the better. The women's suffrage movement, unions and the anti-apartheid movement, among many other initiatives, were all born out of anger at injustice. However, without sufficient resources, the defensive motivational system will drive our anger, resulting in behaviours such as avoiding people, situations or change.

Other emotions with fear at their core include guilt, embarrassment, sadness, panic, grief, regret, defeat, resentment, failure and shame. There are few employees who will say, 'I am resisting this change because I fear that my identity will be lost' or 'I fear the new member of the team is better than me' or the classic, 'I fear failing'. Organisations are more likely to hear employees say: 'I am not sure what this change means for our roles/team' or 'I don't think we should underestimate the importance of experience here' or 'I am not sure that what you are asking is part of my role. I think X should do this activity.'

The Five Cs of Comfort

Understanding fear is a personal journey, digging beneath the surface to examine the source of fear. Some people live their whole life and have no idea where their fears come from, so how are leaders supposed to manage employees' fears when the employees may not understand them themselves?

Luckily, humans have a hard-wired need for a feeling of safety and comfort in five key areas. These areas of comfort have ensured the survival of our species, and we pass on these protective comfort needs from generation to generation. These comfort needs are so critical to our survival that without them we would constantly experience fear.

If we could look inside the Rock of Fear, we would see that our core comfort needs (and therefore source of fear) fall into five categories, all of which stem from the drive to survive.

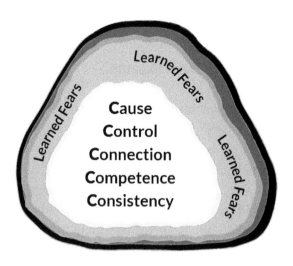

The Rock of Fear

Cause: 'What's the Point?'

To feel safety and comfort we need to know why we do the things we do. We have a limited number of resources – what are we investing them in? A cause provides meaning and purpose. Our cave-dwelling ancestors invested resources in creating tools to feed and defend their families, and there was reward for these efforts. Conversely, to perform an action without knowing why risks loss of time and resources and creates fear.

Control: 'Am I in control?'

We all like to have control over our actions or decisions; after all, putting them in the hands of someone else is a risk. Having a sense of control provides security, and comfort. Being the master of your own destiny provides a sense of safety.

Connectedness: 'Am I likeable?'

Humans are pack animals. There is safety and comfort in numbers. To be ostracised from our cave-community was risky for our ancestors: survival alone was unlikely. We need to feel part of a unit, which is why we create in-groups and out-groups. You are either in my tribe (safe) or in another tribe (a threat). We still have tribes today: football clubs, political parties, music fan groups. The members of our groups are who we identify with, and therefore each group is part of who we are.

Competence: 'Am I good enough?'

Are we capable of dealing with what life throws at us? If we see a challenge that we don't think we have the skills to address, the brain sees that challenge as a threat. Early humans who did not master the art of hunting would starve, so we learned that being competent increases our chances of survival. In today's workplaces, where we are defined by how good we are at our jobs, and rewarded or punished according to our performance, lacking competence can have far-reaching consequences. We therefore need to be seen as capable and competent to gain a sense of comfort. However, some people will go to great lengths to cover their fear that they are not competent.

Consistency: 'Is this familiar?'

Knowing what will happen, or when, gives us a sense of comfort. When something different or out of the ordinary occurs, from a survival perspective the smart thing to do is to assume the new element is a threat – otherwise, the first time our ancestors stumbled across the kitty with the big teeth would have been the last. This is why whenever something unexpected happens, our brain will assume it is a threat. Imagine at 5pm on Friday your boss says, 'I need to see you first thing Monday morning'. If this is not a regularly scheduled meeting, your first emotional response will be: 'Uh oh, this is unusual... What have I done?' You will then spend the rest of the weekend worrying about it.

The need to have comfort in these areas creates 'core' fears. As we move through life we accumulate 'learned' fears. A bad experience at the dentist, being thrown in the swimming pool when you can't swim, the pain of an injection or being laughed at on the playground can all create emotional 'avoid' memories.

The Rock of Fear in the workplace

How do we know what fear an employee is experiencing? Asking questions like 'What are your concerns here?' is superficial, plus the employee themselves may not know. Luckily, people leak the truth. You just need to look and listen for the clues. Consider what the employee values the most. You can often determine this by looking at the resources they invest. If you were forced to choose between relinquishing your home or your car, you are most likely to give up your car, not only because there are more financial resources invested in your home but the home is also a valuable resource to your family, whom you also value. What has your employee invested in the company, processes, systems and their colleagues? The more resources they have invested, the more likely they will be protective, defensive and more resistant to change.

As the head of a talent department for an international company, I invested many resources (money, people, time, emotions, thought, worry, excitement) into piloting a system that would formalise mentoring as a development option across the company. I spent almost a whole year getting the system and processes in place. And it was working! We had some great feedback. However, things changed in the organisation, as they always do. A new leadership team took a different approach and wanted to stop the funding for the programme. My immediate reactions were emotional: anger, disappointment, resentment, guilt (I had involved the whole team in this project) and shame that I had invested so much in something that was now being taken away. This was quite a rip in my balloon.

If I had left it there, my Rock of Fear would have increased size. I would have carried it around for days, weeks and months, letting it deplete my resources as I tried to stay afloat with a tear in my balloon and a big Rock of Fear to carry. But, being a resource-full and SOUND employee, I invested some time in reflecting to understand my responses. I looked at the fear that had driven these emotional responses:

- I was afraid that I had made an incorrect decision in backing the system, which I feared would mean I was incompetent at my job (**competence**).

- I feared my team would see me with less
  authority, which I felt meant I was an incompetent
  leader (**competence, connectedness, control**).

- I feared that if they could get rid of something we
  had invested so much in so easily, they could get
  rid of me just as easily (**connectedness, control**).

I realised if I returned to work the following day and
responded with these beliefs and the huge Rock of
Fear, then my fears would likely come to fruition, but
having a surplus of resources enabled me to apply
logic and cognitive thinking to these fears. There was
no evidence I was an incompetent leader, had less
authority or was going to lose my job; thus, I was able
to plan a thought-through response and start repairing
the tear and shrinking my Rock of Fear.

Did I rescue the programme? No, that was never possible. Not every story has a happy ending, but in having the resources to process cognitively, to look at the
big picture, see alternative views and recognise that it
was my fears that had created my emotions, I was able
to move onwards and upwards. This reflects research
showing that employees with greater resources are
better able to process potentially negative facts in a
systemic way, creating at best a more positive attitude
and an acceptance of the situation at worst.[64]

We all have fears; it's normal. We become masters of
hiding and suppressing our fears and thus function

pretty well despite them. Each employee has a choice as to the extent to which fear drives behaviour, and it is not the remit of an organisation or its leaders to surface and deal with these fears – only the individual can do that. SOUND individuals are already aware of their fears and are busy replenishing their resources and chipping away at their Rock of Fear.

To create SOUND employees, organisations need to acknowledge that fear is a natural part of the human condition, driving behaviour, consciously or otherwise. Organisations can recognise that they have a role to play in enabling employees to RISE by providing and replenishing positive resources, reducing negative resources, and ensuring the environment does not increase their Rocks of Fear. To do this, leaders need to understand the drives and fears of each of their team members: not all fears are equal, and they change over time. My strongest fears used to be connectedness and competence. I wanted to be liked and suffered from imposter syndrome. Moving on in years has brought with it grey hairs but less need to be liked and more confidence in my competence.

There are two strategies to help an employee RISE despite their fears: constantly fill their balloon with the right resources or reduce the size of their Rock of Fear. Preferably, you would do both. Organisations are built around process and structure rather than the nuances of the human brain, and this can unintentionally reduce employees' feelings of safety and their resources. Let's look at how an organisation can maximise employee resources and minimise the Rock of Fear.

QUESTIONS FOR YOUR ORGANISATION

- How psychologically safe do your employees feel? Use the questionnaire in Appendix 1 to find out.
- Can each member of your leadership team answer the following questions about each of their team members:
  - Why do they come to work, other than for pay?
  - Why are they working for your organisation?
  - What inspires them?
  - Where do they want to be in ten years?
  - What are their primary motivators and fears?
  - If they could be anything, what would they be and why?

The answers to these questions are critical if you want to motivate and engage each individual, and they come from knowing the person. What mechanisms are in place in your organisation to foster relationships with employees?

Key learnings from this chapter

- All humans have five core comfort needs that when not met create fear.

- These are protected by our Rock of Fear.

- These comfort needs enable our survival in our environment, even if that environment is the workplace.

PART TWO

CREATING RESOURCE-FULL EMPLOYEES

This part of the book identifies a framework that organisations can apply to create an environment that reduces fear and gives employees sufficient psychological resources to invest in their jobs, the organisation and themselves while also shrinking their Rock of Fear.

The framework is structured around the SAFE acronym, which stands for Story, Arena, Flourish and Ego-lite Ethos.

Feeling SAFE helps an employee RISE

The organisation needs to provide a story, giving meaning to what the employee does so they have a purpose that is bigger than themselves.

Unclear goals and boundaries reduce safety. The employee needs to understand their responsibilities and be able to own them. They need clarity on their own personal arena in which they have accountability and responsibility.

Within the environment, employees should be able to flourish, to grow and develop, not just in line with the company's needs but also according to their needs as individuals.

Finally, companies should operate within an ego-lite ethos – not just as defined by the law but in the values that everyone in the organisation needs to uphold.

The following four chapters will look at each of the SAFE elements in turn: the organisational mechanisms and how the leader implements them.

4
Story

If my long-standing partner decided to surprise me by telling me he was taking us on a last-minute holiday to a secret location, well, I would be surprised. Blooming amazed, actually, but I would go without too many questions. If anyone else tried the same trick, suspicion would set in. I would ask my potential kidnapper for details and maybe I'd put in a call to the nearest police station. I would want to know where we were going, why, who would be there and, of course, what shoes I needed to take with me. I might also want to speak to a few friends, see what they thought, tell them where I was going and make sure they would call the emergency services if they hadn't heard from me within twenty-four hours. The difference? Safety.

I trust that my partner has my best interests at heart. Others may also be looking out for me, but I may need convincing of their motives. It is unlikely (and unprofessional) to develop such a level of intimate trust with your employees; thus, colleagues and bosses fall into the 'others' category. Nothing will make your employees more nervous or suspicious than asking them to go somewhere, or do something, without knowing why and what's in it for them. This is not a selfish response – it's a survival response. To trust anyone outside your inner circle, so much that you would gladly put your life and safety in their hands, is not something that will ensure a continued existence. This means that a key resource for employees is the ability to make sense of what they are doing, where they are going and why.

Organisations need to be clear about where they are going, why, and how they will get there. Importantly, these need to translate into terms that are relevant for the employee: their goals, how they will achieve them and the benefits of success for them. Increasing profit so that shareholders can purchase a yacht for their home in St Tropez is not personal enough.

Research has proven the importance of a clear and credible vision and mission for an organisation. A vision (future aspiration) and mission (current purpose) together can create a gap between purpose and strategic goals that an organisation can fall into. Many organisations also confuse the two terms.[65]

A strong purpose can mitigate many failings in organisations, as those working in the poorly-paid non-profit sector will testify. In an organisation with a meaningful purpose, issues such as politics, game playing and empire building become less important. During the Covid-19 outbreak, I was working with employees of an NHS Trust and they shared with me that they were suddenly able to make decisions and get things done quickly. Meetings that used to take hours now took thirty minutes, and there was less discussion as to who should be responsible for making which decision, or who should action it – it was all about the purpose. When I spoke to employees of a charity that works to support the unemployed, they acknowledged that sometimes the organisation's communications are inconsistent and that the organisation is far from perfect, but what keeps them there, despite knowing they could earn more money elsewhere, is the purpose.

Your organisation's vision and mission can be positive resources for your employees. Not only do they provide direction but they will evoke emotions – hopefully positive ones, such as pride, motivation and enthusiasm. Do your company's vision and mission sound like they've been written by a robot? How do you feel about the following mission:

> 'Enabling our customers to stay ahead of their competition through the provision of quality [insert product/service here]'

This is a typical mission statement – pretty vanilla. Getting your employees to invest their valuable resources in helping another company get better won't inspire them. It would be better to create a mission that evokes an emotion, something employees can be proud to say they are involved in, giving them a purpose to work.

Which of the following example statements evoke emotion: which are you more likely to 'go the extra mile' for?

Table 2: Comparing mission statements

Mission A		Mission B
Enabling our customers to stay ahead of their competition through the provision of quality underwear	or	Making our customers feel comfortable, secure and sexy from underneath
Enabling our customers to stay ahead of their competition through the provision of quality theatre sets	or	Creating atmospheric and moving memories for theatre performers and customers
Enabling our customers to stay ahead of their competition through the provision of quality electric cars	or	Designing and producing high-performing vehicles that create joy for users and the planet
Enabling our customers to stay ahead of their competition through the provision of quality IT security services	or	Making users feel safe by protecting their privacy and personal data through the provision of leading-edge security

The Mission A statements were a bit bland, but notice how the Mission B statements added emotion words: 'comfortable', 'sexy', 'moving', 'joy' and 'safe'.

Of course, you can't just create fantastical visions and missions. Research shows that a key positive resource for employees is a belief that their goals are achievable. Optimism in positive outcomes is a proven predictor of job satisfaction and performance and lower job stress.[66] For our underwear company in Table 2 above, to have a mission to 'Make all our customers a size 6' is as good as not having a mission at all. In fact, a mission or vision that the employee does not consider achievable will provide a negative resource. Working hard for something that they do not believe they can achieve depletes their resources, deflating their balloon, and it can result in denial and disengagement.[67]

Visions can be more of a stretch given they are future aspirations, but the same principle applies: it needs to create passion and positive emotion and be seen as achievable. It is true that not every employee will be proud of or enthusiastic about the company's product or service. Even the most innovative and forward-thinking company will have roles that, although essential, are perceived as unglamorous: data processing, cleaning, parcel delivery, accounting. Each of these jobs has a role to play in achieving the mission and vision; however, if direction and purpose provide positive resources, then it is the leader's role to translate that mission and vision for every team member.

The role of the leader

Can each of your employees articulate how they add value to your organisation and, ultimately, the world around them? What is their purpose? Are they proud of what they do and who they work for?

It is the role of the leader to meaningfully translate the organisation's vision and mission for the employee. Research has shown that employees with meaningful and purposeful work have improved psychological well-being and motivation.[68] Meaning helps create stability and a sense of consistency.[69] A common purpose creates a sense of safety: a horizon that remains fixed, no matter how choppy the sea. It is something employees can focus on to get them through the swell of the waves, when seasickness threatens. When times are rough, our resources are focused on self-preservation and we can lose big-picture thinking, including forgetting the organisation's mission, so leaders need to be able to articulate the purpose of the individual's job role in the context of the mission.

Let's say my role is to put batteries into electric cars. I get the battery, pop it in the relevant slot and connect the wires to it. (Apologies to engineers: I have no doubt it is much more complicated than this, but roll with this as an example.)

The car company's mission is to 'design and produce high-performing vehicles that create joy for users and the planet', but right now I am not feeling much joy, as the demand is high and I am under pressure. Nevertheless, I know that inserting each battery right, first time, is important because it plays a role in saving the planet. And that's important to me because I have three grandchildren and I want to know that they are growing up in a world that will survive longer than they will. Positioning my role in the context of the personal benefits of the organisation's mission provides a bigger purpose and positive resources for me as the employee.

Of course, not all employees have grandchildren, or even children. The leader should know enough about each of their team members to know what's important to them and to communicate the organisation's vision and mission in a way that resonates with each of them. A powerful way to do this is through storytelling.

Stories were originally used to pass information and lessons from generation to generation. Even fairy tales have moral and cultural messages embedded within them. Even if you are not a parent who has spent many hours reading bedtime stories, it is amazing how, decades later, we are still able to remember childhood tales of princesses, dragons, wicked witches and superheroes; yet, remembering what you did at the weekend can be a struggle. The reason is story – or, more specifically, how the brain processes stories.

Traditionally, when organisations wanted to gain buy-in, they provided the facts and figures that supported their decisions, but this is based on the assumption that humans are logical beings. We now know differently: emotions come first and fast. Stories should provide facts, but they also need to generate emotion because the parts of the brain that are involved in emotion generation and processing (the amygdala and hippocampus) are also involved in moving memories from short-term storage to long-term storage. The memories you can most easily recollect are ones that created emotions.

Storytellers articulate messages in a way that engages our hearts first and then our minds.[70] A compelling, relatable narrative generates buy-in and influences others.[71] Stories can help form positive attitudes,[72] although a story designed to create fear can generate emotions just as easily as a story that inspires hope or happiness. In fact, as fear is a survival response, we are more likely to remember events that create negative emotions. One of the academic institutions I work with wanted to keep employees up to date with progress throughout the Covid-19 crisis – and rightly so – but every long, verbose email they sent was full of doom and gloom. Although there were many issues to discuss, the stories being told were only creating negative emotions. The nature and quantity of the emails increased my negative resources so much I began to feel down, panicky and hopeless of a positive outcome. I decided to stop reading these emails for my own mental well-being; thus, the whole purpose of the communication was lost.

Often the best leaders are the best storytellers[73] because they are able to use story to create meaningful connections with goals and roles.[74] Through stories, the leader builds trust. A glimpse into the leader's character helps develop a connection and shared values;[75] as such, storytelling can be an effective tool for influencing and enabling organisational change.[76]

Consider the TV appeals for charity donations. They do not simply present facts such as, 'The number of rough sleepers in England has increased by 15% during 2018';[77] instead, they tell us about a person and their journey. The story will contain relatable elements that generate compassion since studies show that donations are greater when people are emotionally connected to a story.[78]

To communicate a mission for our electric car company, the mission story may describe how the CEO's child developed severe asthma and the journey they went on to discover the impact of car pollution on people, animals and nature. Other factors such as government incentives for the purchase of electric cars to lower carbon emissions are also important, but what employees will remember is the story.

As Simon Sinek says, consider the why.[79] Make your story meaningful. This helps boost employee resources because, when times are tough, the belief that they are doing something positive and meaningful provides positive resources. Job titles run contrary to this idea – they are often convoluted and meaningless. Customers don't care whether you are the Associate to the Executive Manager of Second Tier Solutions, or even Executive Vice President. What is important is not your title but what you *do*. What value you add. Your purpose. Improved titles may be: 'I make IT better for our customers', or 'I create ways for employees to improve'. For our electric car employee, they are not a battery installer, they are a planet crusader!

The power of words

As mentioned in previous chapters, when our fears are triggered our cortisol rises, preparing us for fight or flight. Part of that process involves narrowing our peripheral vision, reducing our hearing and deprioritising our processing brain. This means that once an employee sees or hears something that triggers their fear response, everything else fades into the background. The rest of the message needs to be delivered when they are over the shock and their cognitive brain comes back online.

Communication is a complex business at the best of times, but organisations unwittingly create fear and disable employees' ability to hear the message, and then leaders wonder why people 'just aren't getting it'. Think about the words you use in an announcement and how they may trigger fears. A company annual report I read recently aims to achieve the following in the next twelve to eighteen months:

- Faster innovation through digital transformation

- A simpler, more cost-efficient organisation by harmonising and simplifying our organisational structure

- Returning significant cash to shareholders

I am sure the board members were delighted with this, but what a terrifying message for employees. When employees – particularly those with low resource levels – see 'faster innovation', they interpret it as 'My job is going to be automated' or 'I'll need to be smarter and quicker and I don't know if I can be'. In terms of fears, **control, competence** and **consistency** are all triggered.

'A simpler, more cost-efficient organisation' says one thing: job losses. Any sense of safety is gone. Likewise, 'returning cash to shareholders' means the company needs more profit – ie, cutting budgets and jobs and performing more. Besides, to be honest, only shareholders care about shareholders. All the other good stuff in the report is lost because employees read the above bullet points and their fears are activated, cortisol kicks in and they can't take in the rest.

All in all, this annual statement does not create any safety or comfort for anyone except shareholders and board members. The statements above could have been reworded in ways that quieten our innate fears, as Table 3 shows.

Table 3: Rewording fear-inducing statements

Current fear-inducing statement	Less fear-inducing
Faster innovation through digital transformation.	As part of our drive to [insert organisational purpose/ mission here], we want to better provide [product/ service] to our customers. To do so, we are going to provide employees with improved tools to do their jobs. These include...
A simpler more cost-efficient organisation by harmonising and simplifying our organisational structure.	We will make it easier to work together, eliminating barriers to developing best practice and bringing teams together.
Returning significant cash to shareholders.	We will make our business more cash rich, which will benefit us all by...

Think about the words you use when communicating. Organisational phrases such as 'downsizing', 'increased efficiencies' and 'repurposing' fool no-one. They only awaken employees' fears and remove safety.

QUESTIONS FOR YOUR ORGANISATION

- How do your vision and mission feel? What are the stories behind them?
- Can every employee articulate the organisation's vision and mission? Do they generate positive emotion?
- Can every employee explain their role in the context of the organisation's vision and mission?
- Do your job titles inspire emotion? Is it an emotion that adds to or depletes resources?
- Can each leader tell a story about the importance of their department or function in the context of the vision and mission?

Key learnings from this chapter

💡 Creating meaning and purpose at the level of each employee contributes to their positive cognitive resources.

💡 The part of the brain responsible for 'filing away memories', the hippocampus, also connects these memories to emotions.

💡 If you want someone to remember something, create emotion (preferably a positive one!). Use a story.

💡 The words you use create emotion. Choose them wisely.

5
Arena

Paradoxically, to enable innovation and 'out of the box' thinking you need to provide boundaries and limits.

Remember our 3-metre-long plank spanning across the ten-storey buildings? The fear of crossing the plank narrows your focus, and all your emotions will be focused on your safe passage across it. Physiologically, your heart rate will increase, and cortisol will flood your system, narrowing your peripheral vision and hearing. All your senses are focused on not falling off.

Now, put railings along the plank – or, even better, build a scaffold so the plank doesn't sway in the wind. You are still focused on crossing the plank, but the safety mechanisms mean you can spend fewer resources on not falling, freeing up the resources you had invested in concentrating on where to put your feet. This time, as you cross the plank you may find yourself looking at birds or the view, or enjoying the feel of the wind in your hair. You are present in the moment and absorbing all the surrounding information that crossing the plank can give. You might even notice ways to improve the experience, such as posting signs along the plank telling you about the landmarks you can see. By creating what might seem to be constrictive boundaries, you have opened up the mind.

People cannot think creatively or innovatively while deploying resources on managing perceived threats. For smart thinking, employees need to feel safe.

As organisations strive to become leaner and more agile, they are blurring traditional boundaries between structures, geographies, teams or roles.[80] The popular matrix organisational structure results in more permeable and virtual teams.[81] The security employees once gained as members of a consistent (usually local) team may now be replaced by remote and multiple team membership.[82] Even the 'bedrock' of worker stability, the job description, is increasingly fluid, with imprecise boundaries blurring roles.[83] To maintain organisational flexibility, employment relationships are also becoming more transient, resulting in the 'gig-economy', zero-hour contracts and temporary employment.[84]

Research has shown that loose boundaries lead to poorer team performance.[85] Porous boundaries can result in an increasing workload and uncertainty concerning each task, its outcomes and accountability, creating conflicting priorities for employees and even a perceived threat to professional identity.[86]

A typical matrixed organisation aims to gain consistency by grouping staff according to function and gain flexibility and responsiveness by having staff in regions. The regional employees, however, are in a tough position. One set of instructions comes centrally from their direct boss in HQ, but different instructions come from the regions that often pay for them, and in which they are located. Meanwhile, the regionally mandated work involves a duplication of effort as the Region 1 manager and the Region 2 manager are executing the same task but telling no-one because the task doesn't comply with the HQ request. Each regional manager still has to produce what HQ requires (because HQ will do their performance appraisal) as well as meeting the requirement of the regions.

Furthermore, who is responsible for the outcome of a task or initiative? Accountability is fluid depending on the success of the outcome. The regional managers are doing both the right thing and the wrong thing, depending on perspective, and are expending many resources in managing this ambiguity and the potential threat it entails. What a sad waste of valuable resources.

One of the basic fear triggers is uncertainty (**consistency**). It is safer to assume the unknown is a threat, so we tread cautiously, ready to fight or fly if necessary. Boundaries create a level of certainty, so organisations and leaders need to provide a clear arena in which each employee can operate and manage (**control**).

Defined as 'an enclosure or platform: a sphere or scene of intense activity',[87] an arena is the zone in which the employee has accountability and control. It is clearly demarcated and ringfenced from those of other colleagues. Any areas of intersection are defined, and leaders provide clear roles and responsibilities, eliminating overlap. An arena reduces uncertainty and can increase safety and trust, freeing up valuable employee resources for more constructive activity.[88]

How goals are determined and aligned

Arena clarity is not necessarily dependent on an organisation's structure issue: even in traditional functional structures, clarity of arenas can only be a positive resource for employees. Leaders create a strategy from the strategic gap created by the vision and mission. This filters down to each department, team and employee in the form of roles and goals, and clear goals can create an employee's arena.

The limits of SMART goals

We have all set goals using the well-known SMART acronym devised by Lock and Latham: specific, measurable, agreed, realistic and time bound.[89] This framework helps ensure that team members understand deliverables; yet, in today's ever-changing environment, SMART principles are not enough to create a clear arena. There are several reasons for this.

How SMART goals were set

The creators of the SMART goals principles were advocates of stretch goals, arguing that setting high or difficult goals will 'motivate people to search for new knowledge'.[90] They believed that making the 'S', specificity, of a goal difficult to achieve would lead to high performance, but this was only the case if the employee agreed and accepted the goal. More often than not, goals are presented as a fait accompli. No adults (and few children) like to be told what to do.

It can create a negative emotional response as not being in **control** of what happens to you is a risk to your survival. The loss of control creates fear, which reduces resources and the ability to manage a challenging goal. This supports research findings that only employees with already high levels of resources were in a position to accept challenging goals.[91]

Achievable doesn't mean successful

For employees to feel safe about what they are being asked to do, they need to be clear of the outcome. They need to *feel* that the outcome will be successful – firstly, for them personally (emotions come first) and then, if they have sufficient resources to process beyond emotion, for the business (**competence**). This is not the same as believing an outcome to be achievable: it may be perfectly achievable for the IT manager to phase out the existing operating system, but whether this will lead to a successful outcome for them *as a person* is a different question. Having invested their resources in the existing system for twenty years, the IT manager may fear replacing it with a new system. This fear – fear of the unknown, fear of failure, fear of job loss – will create a tear in their balloon, depleting their resources. The extent to which this loss of resource impacts their performance will depend on how many resources the IT manager had in the first place. If their balloon already had many unrepaired tears, then they would have few resources and their response to the new IT system would remain negative. They'd be unlikely to accept the goal.

An un-agreed goal depletes resources further and the downward spiral continues. If our IT manager had plentiful resources, they may still experience a tear in their balloon (emotional response); however, being resource-full, they can see that the outcome may be successful for the business. They still experience the fear but have the resources to carry that Rock of Fear. The IT manager is now more likely to agree to the goal.

Goals are not just about the outcome

The outcome is only part of the formula for success. As important as a clear and agreed outcome is in setting the arena, employees need to be able to see *how* they can achieve the outcome (**competence, control**). Without the means to achieve it, an outcome is just a dream. To make it real, you need to see the pathways to the successful outcome. I have heard many times in organisations, 'I don't care how you do it, just get it done'. This can lead to ethically ambiguous behaviour and is an example of a leader abdicating and abandoning their responsibility rather than allowing autonomy. This creates panic and fear, resource loss, sinking balloon – you know the drill by now.

Goals provide self-evaluative measures

The SMART framework talks of measurable goals, which is important. It's equally important to recognise that goals provide a self-evaluative measure (**competence**). When you define the outcome and the paths to achieving a goal, employees then evaluate their perceived ability to achieve the goal: their self-efficacy.[92] Note that this is not the employee's actual ability; their perceived ability is what they think they are capable of. There are those who believe that self-efficacy is what enables people to set high personal goals,[93] although others argue that goals lead to self-efficacy,[94] but there is certainly consensus that there is a reciprocal relationship between goals (outcomes and the means to achieve them) and self-efficacy.[95]

Goal setting is a series of evaluative processes. The employee evaluates whether a goal's outcome will be positive for them. If so, they feel optimism, defined as a belief that 'good, rather than bad things will happen and that things will go your way'.[96] Optimism has been linked to happiness, perseverance, achievement, job satisfaction and performance.[97]

The employee's next evaluation is determining whether they have hope: the belief that they can achieve goals, despite any potential obstacles, through pathways and means to meet the goals. If optimism is the 'wish', then hope is the 'willpower' and the 'way-power' to a successful outcome.[98]

Finally, the employee evaluates their self-efficacy: the belief in their ability to achieve the goal.[99] Those with high self-efficacy are more accepting of challenging goals,[100] show more perseverance and effort towards challenging goals,[101] and have improved analytical thinking and problem-solving skills.[102]

If the key to goal setting is the employee's evaluation of the goal, the response to the evaluation is an attitude or belief, which is initially an emotional process. It has to be since emotions come first and fast. Goal setting is therefore not the clinical, logical process that SMART implies. It is emotional, meaning that to ensure the evaluations go beyond the emotional and peripheral processing, employees need resources.

Creating the employee's arena

Remember, the purpose of goals is to achieve the vision and create an arena for the employee, so…

Make it emotional

Despite using SMART, I still find it difficult to meet my goal of going to the gym three times a week to lose 5kg before my summer beach holiday. This goal is specific, it's measurable, I agree (with myself) it needs to be done and it's doable. It is a realistic weight loss and I have a time scale, yet my beach body still evades me as I never seem to get to the gym, finding other critical things to do such as cleaning out the cupboard under the sink.

How can this be? It's a SMART goal! Yes, it is, but it's not an *emotional* goal. The emotion that the thought of an hour-long gym session conjures up is somewhere between boredom and dread. However, if I set the goal in another way, one that attaches me emotionally to the outcome, I am more likely to succeed. Think of all those brides who are suddenly motivated to lose weight for their big day. They have a SMART goal, but it is also emotional. It is all about how they want to feel on that day. If I change my weight loss goal to how I will feel about myself when on the beach and what it means to me, then I am more likely to achieve my SMART goals. Feelings are stronger motivators than logic. If your goal links to a story and a positive emotion, it balances the logic with emotion.

So, in addition to SMART, also use PRIME to create goals that are…

Positively Reframed: Set the goal in a way that encourages people to approach rather than avoid, thereby reducing the chance of a fear response. This means making it positive; rather than 'reducing spend' you are 'increasing margins'.

Intrinsically Motivated: What is the drive to achieve the goal? Not an extrinsic reward like commission. Money is only a limited motivator; it's what money can bring that is the motivator. It's not the bonus or commission, it's the family holiday, the new hot tub, the latest sports car... they are the motivators because they have emotion attached to them.

Emotive: Recognise what positive emotions achieving the goal will bring. What will the goal mean to the individual, their identity, who they are? How will it feel when you have that new sports car? What will a family holiday mean to your kids/partner?

Make it collaborative

Collaboration can be tough if, for example, the president or CFO has decreed that all budgets need to be cut by 5%. No-one negotiated that with you, and you have no choice in the matter, but you are a leader and that is part of your role, as is motivating, managing and engaging your team. Therefore, your approach needs to be collaborative.

Whether you make the budget cuts as a team or one on one, employees need to feel that what you are asking is achievable. They also need some autonomy in setting the goal. This also means that you may need to negotiate over several meetings.

Take time

By holding the goal discussion over more than one meeting, the employee is less likely to feel that the goal was foisted upon them. Having a two-way discussion increases their sense of autonomy.

Depending on how volatile the situation is and the amount of change happening in your organisation, it may be better to set the goals over small periods of time, indicating that they can be adjusted if need be. The employee will be more likely to commit to a short-term goal than a longer-term goal in a changing environment.

Set the boundaries of the arena

The contents of the goals need to define the employee's arena: they need to provide boundaries in terms of their role and responsibilities. This relates to the 'specific' aspect of SMART; however, the specificity might need to include what's out of scope, who the employee has to help and include, what their level of authority is and key relationships. A stakeholder analysis can also be useful here. The role and goals need to set the arena that the employee can play in and control.

Create accountability

Having created a clear arena for your employee, detailing their responsibilities, scope and goals, you are now in a strong position to hold them accountable. If the employee has agreed to the goal and feels that they are able to achieve a successful outcome, then they will have no problem with taking account-ability. If there is any 'squirming' from the employee about being held to account, this is a signal that they feel doubt or fear. Work through it, and accountability will come.

Letting an employee know that they will be held accountable is like a boundary. If implemented well, it provides a sense of safety, an understanding of expectations. Boundaries give children emotional security; so too with adults. How many times have you heard 'I like working with them because I know where I stand with them'? Even if you are standing on the wrong side of them, at least you know and don't have to guess. Accountability defines expectations and the arena in which the employee is expected to perform.

Accountability also provides safety because the employee knows that you will be holding others to account for their deliveries as well. A fair approach to performance creates a sense of safety because it means consistency. Unfairness generates uncertainty and the unknown, which means fear.

A note here on the leader's accountability. Although you may create a clear arena for the employee, the politics, empire building and power struggles that are inevitable in any environment where physical resources are scarce may encroach on the employee's arena. Your role as a leader is to protect the employee's arena and be a champion for them, freeing them from such distractions so they can focus on their arena. Where another employee or leader makes a bid for you or your employee's arena, *you* need to publicly hold the interloper to account. As Perry Belcher, co-founder of Digitalmarketer.com says: 'Nothing will kill a great employee faster than watching you tolerate a bad one.'

I have spent over thirty years in organisations, and I am amazed at how often managers fail to hold colleagues to account for poor performance or poor behaviour. Leaders and employees are constantly dealing with the consequences of it, yet they will not deal with it directly. This is weak management.

In one organisation, the purchasing department's arena was to identify, assess and negotiate with potential suppliers to meet an internal customer's need. The purchasing department would then whittle the field down to two or three potential suppliers, at which point the business requester would help in the final selection process to ensure that suppliers met robust criteria, prices could be negotiated and costs controlled. The purchasing department had a clear arena: they knew who they serviced, what they provided, how they contributed to the organisation's success and that they were experts at their jobs. However, other departments would often present the purchasing department with their chosen supplier having already signed a contract with them. The other department's manager had encroached into the arena of the purchasing department.

As a consequence, those in purchasing felt threatened and worried that they were not needed (**connectedness**). They felt angry because they weren't able to do their jobs properly and they felt stressed that this affected their ability to meet their goals of managing the budget due to departments 'spending' without approval (**competence**). Each of these feelings were sapping the department's resources, causing negativity, and what made it worse was that leaders were allowing it to happen. The purchasing leader wasn't protecting their team's arena and the leaders flaunting the process were tolerated. The purchasing department felt cynical about leaders and found it unfair that some people were allowed to circumvent the process with no consequence (**consistency**). No-one held these mavericks accountable for their behaviour.

Accountability is equally relevant at job level. Finding out someone else is doing what you are supposed to do throws up fear, negative feelings and disengagement. Your role as a leader is to hold those who encroach on others' arenas accountable and deal with the encroachment. In doing so, you establish boundaries for the department's, team's or employees' arenas and practise fairness, which provide safety, adding to each employee's positive resources. And ironically, when employees within departments feel safe, they are more open to collaborate and engage with others.

Setting your employees up for success

Your role as a leader is to set people up for success; therefore, where possible, provide whatever they need to achieve a goal. Often the employee, being the expert at their job, will know what they can do with the time, money, technology and people available, which is where negotiation comes in. However, simple things can often set employees up for success and add to their positive resources.

Facebook has a philosophy of 'If you need it to perform your job, then take it'. They have a gadget vending machine in which items such as phone chargers, USB sticks, pens, batteries, computer mice and even headphones are available. You swipe your employee card, and the item gets dispensed and charged to your cost centre. No need for forms, authorisations or grovelling to the keeper of the supply cupboard key. If you need a USB stick to perform your job, then take it. Not only does this treat employees like adults (thus adding to their resources) and displaying trust (also adding to resources), it also sends a message that the company wants to enable you to succeed.

Different people might need different things, such as the option to work from home, finish at 4pm, work from another office, have a standing desk or receive training. I appreciate these are small things (to you) and you have 'real' problems to deal with, but look at it this way: if they need these small things to perform, then give them to your employee. The absence of these 'small things' can create a huge loss of resource – then it becomes a big thing.

Companies fear abuse here, but if employees are truly held accountable for their arenas and deliveries there will be minimal abuse of such systems. And where there is abuse, the employee will be held accountable for that too.

In today's VUCA environment, sometimes we are set goals that seem 'impossible' for us to achieve. And when unfamiliar issues occur, we cannot even assume that the leader knows what needs to be done. In fluid environments, goals are unclear or may change often or unexpectedly.[103] For employees with high resources, these are challenges to overcome; for employees with few resources, they are a source of stress. In such an environment, the goal-setting process is key. It needs to give the employee hope and optimism, increasing the resources they have to evaluate goals.

As discussed earlier in this chapter, one thing an employee evaluates is their own self-efficacy: are they capable of achieving the goal? One of the greatest contributors to employee resources – and employee success – is the opportunity to gain new skills and knowledge. The employee needs to be able to flourish.

QUESTIONS FOR YOUR ORGANISATION

- Can each leader and manager set goals that link to the mission story? How are emotional goals created?
- What mechanisms are in place to define clear employee arenas?
- How are people held accountable? How is conflict dealt with?
- To what extent is your goal-setting process collaborative? How does it add to or deplete employee resources?
- Is each employee able to articulate their arena and its boundaries?
- Looking at your goal-setting (and other) processes, to what extent do they provide hope, optimism and self-efficacy and personal meaning?

Key learnings from this chapter

💡 Help employees feel safe by creating boundaries; an arena in which they are responsible and accountable.

- Intrinsic motivation is far more powerful than extrinsic motivators. Create goals that are both logical and emotional using SMART and PRIME.

- Set people up for success, give them what they need. If what they need is too big or not possible, collaborate to find a solution.

- Hold people to account.

6
Flourish

One of the wonderful things about young children is their belief that they can do anything. Their lack of inhibition and fear makes everything possible. Everything they do receives praise, and at that age there are a lot of 'firsts' to celebrate: their first word, their first steps, the first successful use of the potty. Their Rock of Fear is grit-sized since they were born with only two innate fears: the fear of falling and the fear of loud noises. They have not yet had the experiences that develop the quarry-load of fears that adults carry around. Their self-efficacy is high – which is why they need parents to make sure they don't emulate Superman off the garage roof.

As children head off to school, rewards become conditional and they develop their sense of self in comparison with peers. Children may learn to be competitive, feeling negative emotions when they don't come first in the egg-and-spoon race, are the top of the class in maths or graduate with a First. Some schools are more enlightened in this regard, but I can still remember being asked why I wasn't as good at running the 100m as my sister. She was labelled 'the sporty one' and I 'the brainy one'. These labels stuck and defined our paths in life, which is unfortunate, because she is equally as 'brainy' as I am, although I am not as sporty as her… or, rather, I *believe* I am not as sporty. This belief is nonsense because our bodies are equally capable. As parents, we also do our best with the resources we have, but our behaviour shows our children what to believe about themselves and the world. By the time our children join the workforce, they have had a plethora of experiences that defined their belief, or lack of belief, in their capabilities: their self-efficacy.

The capability of self-efficacy

Self-efficacy has been associated with coping and resilience and is a key mechanism in dealing with life's challenges, from childhood adversity to pregnancy, relationships and bereavement.[104] This is no surprise given the need for **competence** to alleviate fears. In the workplace, a strong relationship between self-efficacy and performance has been demonstrated,[105] showing those with high self-efficacy were more accepting of challenging goals, showed more perseverance and effort towards high or chal-lenging goals and had improved quality of analytical thinking and problem solving. Particularly relevant for today's environments, self-efficacy has been shown to moderate the stress of ambiguity in the workplace.[106]

Having employees with high self-efficacy can only benefit the organisation. While it is not the role of the organisation to unpick any life experiences that have led to an employee's low self-efficacy, nor is it their role to reduce self-efficacy, the organisation and its leaders have the gift of being able to increase an employee's self-efficacy. This is critical for performance because when an employee evaluates their likelihood of achieving a goal (optimism) and the pathways to achieving the goal (hope), they do so *through the lens of self-efficacy*. The employee is not thinking 'Is this goal achievable?' but 'Is this goal achievable *for me?'*

		Protest, activism	Action
Self-efficacy	High	*'I don't think so. That's not happening and here is why.'*	*'Sure, no problem. I'll get to it.'*
		Apathy, resignation	**Self-devaluation, despondency**
	Low	*'Whatever. No point in arguing.'*	*'Everyone else could do this, but not me.'*
		Low	High
		Optimism (outcome judgement)	

Self-efficacy and optimism[107]

Bandura, the godfather of self-efficacy, illustrates this lens in a four-box model. Whether the employee sees the outcome of the goal as achievable or not, their response to the goal will depend on their self-efficacy. Those with high self-efficacy will either start working on the goal or they will confidently tell you why they can't. An employee with low self-efficacy will respond negatively, whether they see the goal as achievable or not. How an employee perceives their self-efficacy will impact their performance, so what are the barriers to self-efficacy and how do we reduce them?

Think of all the events in your life that created your sense of efficacy: getting a degree, being promoted or even something as simple as assembling your latest IKEA purchase. Similarly, failing to achieve also shapes your belief about your self-efficacy. Being told I was not a sporty student impacted my perception of my ability to do sport, and I dealt with my perceived lack of competence in all things sporty by simply not doing them – my gym kit was always 'forgotten'. Inputs from parents, teachers, friends and even society in general can impact us emotionally and create beliefs that may not be true, despite the evidence. We remember the events that created an emotional response.

Given we spend most of our waking hours at work, it is a major contributor to our self-efficacy. We invest many resources into work, so it becomes an environment against which we measure our self-efficacy. Building and maintaining employee resources is an organisation-wide effort, and this chapter is about those efforts – in particular, how to make the most of the 'return vs learn' decision.

This chapter is not going to tell you to give people the training they need to do their job. You know this already. Admittedly, though, training is often under-valued or ignored. Your employees need the opportunity to gain the knowledge and skills to succeed; after all, your role as a leader is to set them up for success.

There are some great examples of enlightened organisations that recognise the importance of enabling employees to learn. Jaguar Land Rover offers each of its employees an opportunity to learn something non-work related – the employee can learn cake decorating or basket weaving if they want to. As long as the employee is learning and growing, they are building their self-efficacy, increasing their resources and therefore enabling better work performance.

Research has shown that the wider your range of knowledge and experience, the more creative you can be.[108] Consider how many great ideas have been the result of adapting products and processes from other industries. 3M developed a new concept for preventing post-surgical infections from the field of theatrical make-up.[109] Old-school leaders will say, 'What if the employee takes a course and then leaves as a result?' To this, I would say that it takes more than a course for someone to give up a job that they enjoy and that replenishes their resources. If they leave, then they were going to leave anyway because they were not committed or engaged, and that's a leadership failure. Overall, the benefits of this type of extracurricular learning outweigh any risks.

If people need skills developed, train them – this helps set them up for success. If you don't, their job may sap their hope, optimism and self-efficacy every day, creating multiple tears in their balloon. You will end up with an employee that is permanently operating in a defensive and emotional state, which is no fun for anyone.

While training and development is important, sending someone on a course does not automatically mean they are developing, growing or flourishing. Nor do courses compensate for systemic structural and cultural mechanisms that sap self-efficacy and resources. Flourishing is not about training; it's about creating an environment that builds on an employee's self-efficacy, both personally and professionally.

Return vs learn

Whichever project management methodology your organisation uses, they all have a phase during which reflection should take place. It is usually during the 'closing' phase and is called something like 'lessons learned' or 'review'. The time and effort invested into these actions varies. Often, the project manager and team are deployed onto the next project before any review takes place, or, if there was a review, the document was filed away, lost in time and space in a little-used shared drive.

Taking time out to reflect and review does require time and space, both of which business demands can swallow. To learn, we need to reflect. Otherwise, as we often find in project management, the same mistakes are made over and over again.

Kolb developed the experiential learning cycle to describe how we learn from experience.[110] This cycle shows that much of our learning comes from experiences that don't go as planned. If I have a big argument with my friend, emotions run high, tempers are lost, words are spoken that shouldn't have been, and there are lots of tears on both sides. After the argument, I go through a process of reflection in which I deploy cognitive resources to think and consider the event. I can then rationally draw a conclusion as to what happened and why, and I practise what I will say when I next see my friend and what I will say if the topic arises again. When I see my friend again, I am able to apply this practice, which gives me an experience, which may be good or bad… and the cycle continues. In this way, we iteratively learn and grow.

Without the reflection process, whether personally or at work, we are less likely to learn. We will keep wondering why the same thing keeps happening to us. If we don't reflect, we don't learn – we stay the same. In our hot-air balloon model, the reflection takes place at the point of 'return vs learn', where an individual decides or is enabled to learn from an experience. But an employee can only invest resources in reflection and learning if they have sufficient resources to do so. Organisations can support this process by providing employees with the time, resources and mechanisms to choose to learn, rather than return.

Organisational learning refers to processes or activities that provide new information or knowledge and are individual-focused.[111] Flourishing goes beyond that. Flourishing happens in environments where learning is a culture – a mindset that applies to all employees at all hierarchical levels.[112] These environments lead to improved organisational performance[113] through increased innovation, effective change,[114] job satisfaction,[115] team relationships[116] and employee self-efficacy.[117]

How do leaders lead in a way that enables flourishing? It's all about allowing the employee to 'do' and to 'think'.

Doing

Leaders will argue that they already let people 'do'. In fact, they may even want employees to 'do' more. But learning and flourishing from doing is not about what you do – it's about how you do it.

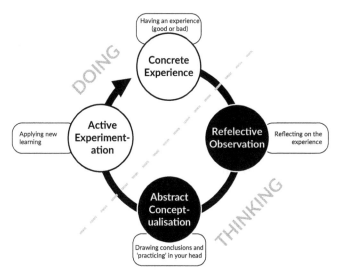

Experiential learning cycle, adapted from D.A. Kolb (1984)

During the industrial revolution and rise of the factories, people were employed not for their brains but for their brawn. They were taught how to perform a single task and required to perform it over and over again. Once the skill was learned, execution began and that was the end of employee development. The factory needed nothing more from that employee.

These days, we look to employ people who add value to our organisation: people who can work with others, fit in with the company culture and actively contribute to growing the business. In the 'knowledge economy', we employ people for their brains. Some tasks still need to be performed consistently each time, especially in compliance-orientated industries such as finance and medicine, but even within those frameworks organisations look for people who can improve operations.

Often, the people you hire know more about the process, technology or subject than you do, so let them flourish. The leader's role is no longer about telling people what to do; if that's why you want to be a leader, you are in the wrong job. You and your ego need to go elsewhere (see Ego-Lite Ethos chapter). Telling people what to do makes you at best a manager (not a leader), at worst a bully. The leader's role is to enable the employee to work out the task themselves, providing just enough guidance to help them develop self-efficacy. This teaches employees what they are capable of. After all, it doesn't matter how many people tell you that you are good at something – you only believe it when you see it for yourself.

Not everyone has the same ability or motivation to complete tasks and add value, and the leader needs to enable all employees – from the newly hired graduates to the close-to-retirement long server – to flourish. Speaking as an old dog myself, yes, we can be taught new tricks. Leaders need to adapt their styles depending on the employee's ability and willingness. The amount of autonomy and instruction a leader provides lies along a continuum: the more willing and able the employee, the more autonomy you can give, and the less instruction and checking up needed.

Nothing will sap an employee's resources more than being left to do something they can't do. That is not autonomy, it is abandonment. The employee will feel overwhelmed, causing tears in their balloon and undermining their self-efficacy and resilience. Similarly, there is nothing that will sap your resources (and patience) like being told how to do something you are already perfectly capable of, like when your partner instructs you on how to load the dishwasher – a task you have performed daily for the past twenty years. It is a waste of everyone's time and causes unnecessary conflict.

Hersey and Blanchard's Situational Leadership model demonstrates the differing styles that can be used depending on an individual's ability and willingness.[118] Although their model suggests that coaching is the appropriate style for those who are willing and able, I would argue that, to create a learning organisation, coaching is key to addressing *all* of the situations, adjusting the focus for each. While developing leaders who coach is beyond the scope of this book, if you would like help using coaching to manage your employees' development and performance, contact me via the links at the back of the book.

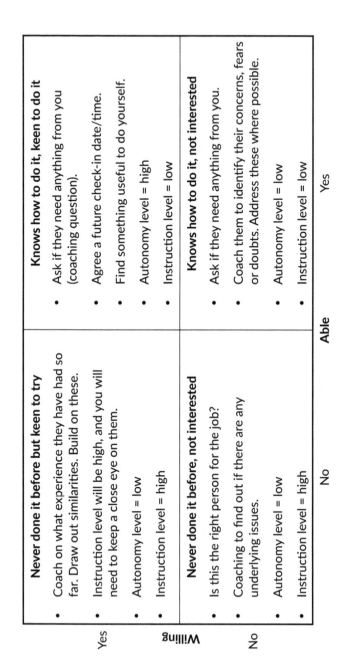

	Never done it before but keen to try	**Knows how to do it, keen to do it**
Yes	• Coach on what experience they have had so far. Draw out similarities. Build on these. • Instruction level will be high, and you will need to keep a close eye on them. • Autonomy level = low • Instruction level = high	• Ask if they need anything from you (coaching question). • Agree a future check-in date/time. • Find something useful to do yourself. • Autonomy level = high • Instruction level = low
Willing		
	Never done it before, not interested	**Knows how to do it, not interested**
No	• Is this the right person for the job? • Coaching to find out if there are any underlying issues. • Autonomy level = low • Instruction level = high	• Ask if they need anything from you. • Coach them to identify their concerns, fears or doubts. Address these where possible. • Autonomy level = low • Instruction level = low
	No	**Yes**
	Able	

Examples of differing leadership styles based on the Situational Leadership Model
by Hersey and Blanchard

Coaching is an essential leadership tool because it helps creates an environment of learning. It enables employees to 'do' and 'think'. If you don't do, then you won't have an experience from which to learn and flourish. And if you don't think about what you did, you won't learn from it.

What if you allow your employee to 'do' and they fail? Well, let's talk about failure.

Do you feel the need to provide detailed instructions and closely monitor employees because you don't believe they will get it right – or worse, they won't do it the way you would? Do you feel the need to **control** the process and make sure it is done as per your instructions? This is your Rock of Fear talking, or its potentially malevolent cousin, ego, which we'll talk more about in the Ego-Lite Ethos chapter. For now, let us stick with failure.

How do you and your organisation deal with failure? Is the response to find the person responsible? Is there a belief that failure is a result of incompetence and laziness? Is failure met with 'punishment' such as low appraisal ratings or a lack of promotion? A culture that treats 'failures' this way adds to the Rock of Fear. People are afraid of doing something wrong, and this results in a downward spiral:

- A portion of an employee's resources is being invested in covering their tracks rather than on the job in hand, therefore…

- The employee's resources are reduced, therefore...

- The employee is operating in defensive mode, therefore...

- They lack the ability and willingness to take risks, come up with new ideas or challenges, therefore...

- Their enjoyment of their job decreases, therefore...

- Their resources deplete, therefore...

- They have fewer resources...

And so the spiral continues – for the employee and you, their leader.

'Ridiculous!' you exclaim. 'This is the twenty-first century. We gave up public floggings and pay docking after that BBC exposé.' Perhaps it's worth reiterating that the brain sees any perceived threat as a punishment. For an employee who feels that they are not good enough (**competence**), 'feedback' can be a punishment. For the employee who feels guilt about not spending more time at home with the children (**control, cause**), having to work extra hours can be a punishment. For an employee with a high need to be liked (**connectedness**), an off-the-cuff comment from their leader about their 'failure' can be a punishment. Even training can be seen as a punishment if you position a course as part of a 'performance improvement plan', typical of learning provision in organisations.

Let us start by taking the fear out of failure by reframing it as feedback. I can see some of you rolling your eyes, picturing me hugging a tree, but think about it. If you get something wrong and 'fail', that failure is merely feedback that you need to do something differently. Thinking this way is part of a 'growth mindset', a concept developed by Carol Dweck.[119] It can reframe negative events into positive development opportunities, replenishing rather than depleting resources.

Before reading any further, you might want to complete the growth mindset questionnaire in Appendix 2 to help you determine where you are on the continuum between a fixed and growth mindset. We generally have a bit of both in us – after all, we are not the finished article yet.

A growth mindset culture acknowledges that everyone can learn and grow. This mindset reframes attitudes about abilities, failures, obstacles and feedback in a way that maintains rather than depletes resources and lightens the Rock of Fear.

Table 4: Fixed vs growth mindset

Fixed Mindset		Growth Mindset
Knowledge and skills are fixed traits.	Vs	Knowledge and skills can grow with time and effort.
Either you have talent, or you don't.	Vs	Talent is effort (inspiration + perspiration); we can all develop it.
It's a dog-eat-dog world.	Vs	Creating win-win scenarios adds value for both parties.
Needing to improve is a sign of weakness.	Vs	No-one is the finished article.
Strong judgements: right/ wrong, good/bad, black/ white.	Vs	There is good/bad, right/ wrong in everything. There are always grey areas.
Jealous of others' success.	Vs	Inspired by others' success: What can I learn?
Failure is bad.	Vs	There is no such thing as failure, only feedback.
Doesn't want to make mistakes.	Vs	Sees mistakes as opportunities.
Avoids challenges: they may expose weaknesses.	Vs	Challenges are opportunities to learn and grow. If I don't know it, I can learn it.

Whereas a fixed mindset results in taking a binary approach to evaluating situations or ourselves as 'right' or 'wrong' or 'good' or 'bad', which may impact self-esteem and self-efficacy, a growth mindset improves motivation, perseverance and self-efficacy.[120]

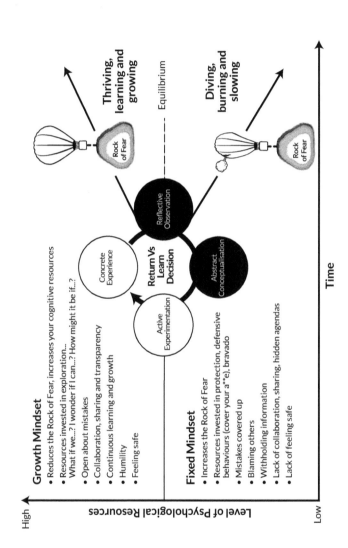

Growth Mindset
- Reduces the Rock of Fear, increases your cognitive resources
- Resources invested in exploration... What if we...? I wonder if I can...? How might it be if...?
- Open about mistakes
- Collaboration, sharing and transparency
- Continuous learning and growth
- Humility
- Feeling safe

Fixed Mindset
- Increases the Rock of Fear
- Resources invested in protection, defensive behaviours (cover your a**e), bravado
- Mistakes covered up
- Blaming others
- Withholding information
- Lack of collaboration, sharing, hidden agendas
- Lack of feeling safe

Concrete Experience

Active Experimentation

Return Vs Learn Decision

Reflective Observation

Abstract Conceptualisation

Rock of Fear

Thriving, learning and growing

Equilibrium

Rock of Fear

Diving, burning and slowing

Level of Psychological Resources

High

Low

Time

Impact of a growth mindset on the Rock of Fear

Believing that learning is lifelong enables us to choose to see 'mistakes' as opportunity for learning, rather than a cause for punishment, and sends a message that it is safe to try new things. This leads to increased resources and a smaller Rock of Fear, enabling thriving, learning and growing. Mitigating core fears is critical for flourishing. Employees who subdue these fears have the resources to invest in learning and flourishing.

I am not suggesting you create a Pollyanna 'soft and fluffy' organisation. If one individual is compromising the growth of another employee, a team or the organisation, then the right thing to do is to provide the individual with feedback to give them an opportunity to grow and change.[121] Should the employee choose not to take this opportunity, you may need to remove them from the organisation.

People make mistakes, and it is unrealistic to expect perfection from anyone, including yourself. Failure itself is not the issue; it's how the organisation, leader and employee deal with failure. If you get something wrong and 'fail', evaluate what you need to do differently – which is where the 'thinking' part comes in…

Thinking

The enlightened leader knows that mistakes lead to learning, improvements and innovations. Many great inventions were accidents: penicillin, Post-It notes, Play-Doh and others that don't begin with 'P' (such as microwaves, Teflon and saccharin).

Mistakes can be opportunities to learn. Note: this is not about failing repeatedly at the same thing. Indeed, if this is happening, then clearly there is no learning taking place! To positively reframe mistakes, you need to spend time reflecting and thinking about them. You can't change past events, but you can change what happens in the future.

Reflecting on issues can take place subconsciously. If you consider when our best ideas come to us, when solutions to problems magically appear, it is often when we are not thinking about them. It could be when we are driving home, playing an instrument, even exercising. From a neuroscience perspective, gaining 'insight' – that 'aha' moment – is the point when information from diverse areas of the brain come together to create a solution or a realisation. At this point the brain frequency hits >25 Hz (waves per second): gamma waves, however this moment of insight often occurs during a theta state, when our brain waves are operating at a much more sedate 4–8 Hz (waves per second). The theta frequency can be reached through meditation, when the brain is almost in 'neutral'. It can also be achieved through activities in which you become so absorbed that you are not analysing what you're doing, you are just going with the flow. You may be in this mental state after the first 3km of a run (the first 3km is always hell) or when you are playing music or letting your mind wander and daydream. Sometimes it is when you first wake up because during sleep your unconscious will have been processing. 'Sleeping on it' remains good advice for problem solving.

The processes of doing (and practising doing where possible) and reflection are key to learning.[122] Apart from ensuring that employees have time off for rest and recuperation, there are also tangible ways to encourage such reflection and learning in the workplace. Leaders can spend time coaching the employee to reflect on an event, learn from it and plan for the future. A check in with employees about how they feel, what they are learning and how you can help them can be a five-minute conversation or a series of long conversations over the course of a career – preferably both. As a result, flourishing becomes integral to the organisation. Learning is not one-off training but a continuous and evolutionary process.

Organisations might consider structuring meetings or training events to enable reflection. Providing an agenda before and a follow-up opportunity after would allow individuals to reflect on what they are going to say and what they said.

Offices are becoming more open plan, yet this has been shown to cause distraction and stress.[123] Persistent distractions and noise can reduce our ability to focus, while providing quiet spaces allow employees to step away and think. I worked for one company that provided 'sleep pods', where you could go at any time to close your eyes, listen to music, meditate or take a power nap. A breakout area by the kitchen had a TV and a PlayStation and was furnished with bean bags so people could relax and socialise during breaks.

These forward-thinking initiatives, sadly, did not have the desired effect. The sleep pods were on the same floor as the offices of the executives, who considered the need for breaks during the day unnecessary and 'weak'. The breakout room was abandoned after an incident when an individual was playing computer games *during his break* and was yelled at to return to his desk as work was piling up. This only happened once, but word gets around. The breakout room became a monument to misalignment of intent and leadership style. Organisations can proudly show their employee benefits, such as well-being programmes, gyms, lunchtime meditations and massages, but they are meaningless if leaders don't support them by believing in them. How leaders lead – leadership ethos – determines whether people flourish or not.

QUESTIONS FOR YOUR ORGANISATION

- What are the consequences of an individual making a mistake?
- What processes are in place to allow reflection?
- How do leaders enable learning?
- How is coaching practised in the workplace? Is it constructive coaching or inspection?
- What's your learning mindset? Try filling in the questionnaire in Appendix 2.

Key learnings from this chapter

💡 Those with a healthy functioning brain can learn anything.

💡 Learning increases your general sense of self-efficacy.

💡 To reach moments of insight and creativity, sometimes you need to stop thinking about the problem.

💡 Adopting a growth mindset provides opportunities to learn from, not suffer for mistakes.

💡 There is no such thing as failure, only feedback!

💡 Learn to coach.

7
Ego-Lite Ethos

An ethos is: 'The fundamental character or spirit of a culture. The underlying sentiment that informs the beliefs, customs or practices of a group or society: dominant assumptions of a people or period.'[124] Leaders help shape the ethos of their organisation.

I often ask leaders: 'Why did/do you want to be a leader?' Their answers can be telling. What would your answer be? Consider some of the reasons below – maybe circle a few.

Status	Salary	Validate your worth		Benefits	Authority	Expected of me	Be the boss
Perks	Grow self	Influence	Learn	Mentor	Autonomy	Support	Competition
Career	Prestige	Success	Coach	Do the fun stuff	Climb the corporate ladder	Connect	Recognition
Control	Serve	Legacy	Enable	Be in charge	Bigger car	Contribute	Gain higher peers
Grade	Power	Determine direction		Title	Delegate boring stuff		Promotion

These drivers contribute to the ethos of an organisation, more so than any list of company values, because they are the drivers that inform behaviour. How we lead depends on our beliefs about what leadership is. Research has shown that the style of leadership is a big factor in whether people feel safe at work[125] – whether they feel 'able to show and employ one's self without fear of negative consequences to self-image, status or career'.[126]

It's not just about your leadership style, though. You may be the perfect leader (if there is such a thing), but seeing another, less-than-perfect, leader in action can impact your team's sense of safety. Remember, it only took one leader to yell at the unsuspecting gamer in my former employer's breakout room for all staff to abandon it. It's one for all and all for one when it comes to leaders developing an environment in which employees feel safe enough to invest resources in smart thinking rather than protective mechanisms. A common ethos is needed: an ego-lite ethos.

Ego

The ego gets a bad rap, but there is no point deriding it as we all have one. That's why I argue for an ego-lite, not an ego-free, organisation. As psychologists will tell you, the whole notion of the ego is complex – some may talk about the ego, the superego, the id or the shadow self – but for the purposes of helping people build and maintain their resources, let's keep it simple. Ego means 'I' and is formed of the beliefs you have about yourself. These self-beliefs can be positive or negative, and most people have some combination of both. The ego's job is to satisfy our wants and needs to bring us benefit rather than grief, which is why *all* behaviour is beneficial. I'll give you a minute to ponder that.

When I mention this in my leadership programmes, there is always someone who disagrees, leading to great discussion. 'How can all behaviour be beneficial?' they say. 'What about murderers?'

In the healthy human brain, the ego makes sure that we move away from grief, pain and harm and towards comfort, safety or benefit. It is another one of those handy survival mechanisms. Even murderers, *at the moment they commit the crime*, are getting some benefit from it: perhaps a release of rage, jealousy, power or sexual gratification. I can't speculate on specific motives; I am not a murderer.

Let us take a more common example: smoking. People know that smoking is bad for them, yet they still do it. Why? Because it provides some kind of benefit. Ask a smoker what benefit it brings and they will cite time away from their desk, time to think, a social moment or relaxation. All behaviour is beneficial *for that person*. Even the most annoying and difficult person you work with, their behaviour has a benefit for them. Understand what that benefit is and you will be able to understand their behaviour – and then manage it.

Ninety-nine times out of 100, the benefit gained from a behaviour is to protect the individual from pain. The pain can be either physical or emotional: the brain treats them the same. The biggest cause of emotional pain is fear, so think of the ego as a protective wrapping around our Rock of Fear.

Being vulnerable and open about emotional pain is slowly becoming more acceptable. The rise in awareness of mental health issues and recognition that they can affect anyone is becoming more mainstream. Good thing, too. Traditionally, we were expected to hide our fears and vulnerabilities. We did not walk around swinging our Rock of Fear in public for all to see. Like genitals, we all have a Rock of Fear but only a select few ever see it. We spend a lot of time, effort and resources hiding the Rock of Fear. In some organisations, we may not feel safe exposing our fears. Just as we cover our nakedness with clothes, we each cover our Rock of Fear using a wrapping called 'ego'.

How we wrap our Rock of Fear will depend on our self-beliefs, fears, upbringing and experiences. But the purpose of the ego wrapping is the same for all: to protect us. It is the nature of the wrapping that will influence how we interact with the outside world.

Consider your ego as an army, a line of soldiers protecting you from anything that might stimulate a fear or shake your self-belief. Your fears or self-belief could be unfounded, but the army doesn't care. They are trained to protect the Rock of Fear and associated self-beliefs, and they will respond immediately by deflecting, attacking, standing down or disarming any inputs.

Some say that attack is the best form of defence. When our army senses our fears are awakening, it attempts to prevent this, and the associated pain, by attacking. We can see this in arguments when people say, 'Well, it was your fault because you did X'. It's also a common approach for political parties: attack the opponent, and hopefully the people won't notice our deficiencies.

The Ego Army does let some stimuli through. Anything that is positive and will support our self-beliefs (whether they are right or wrong) gets a free pass. Sometimes this means disarming comments so that they align with our self-beliefs. Misalignment between what we see or hear and our self-perception can cause pain (and use up resources). The Ego Army might disarm negative comments, turning them into less negative ones by taking the 'ammunition' out of them. The army may respond to negative comments by adding thoughts like 'They are jealous of my success' or 'I am just too intelligent for them' or 'They are idiots'.

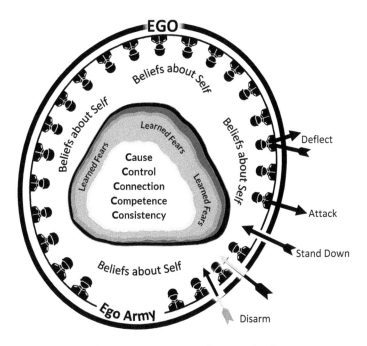

The Ego Army responding to stimuli

Similarly, the Ego Army may disarm positive comments, turning them into negative ones because a negative version of the comment aligns with our self-belief. The Ego Army may disarm a compliment like 'Good job' by thinking, 'It was luck, not skill'.

Some people have extensive Ego Armies, perhaps even deploying two layers in areas of particular vulnerability. At the other end of the spectrum is an Ego Army with few soldiers – only a few Ego Sentries posted at key areas of vulnerability. Their role is to watch, acknowledge and report back to you. You then decide whether to allow in or deflect the positive and negative inputs. To make this decision, you must reflect to determine what inputs are relevant and how they may be helpful. You may receive great praise but choose to deflect it because it is from someone who has an ulterior motive. Conversely, you may let in negative input because, although it initially causes pain, in the long run it provides you with more knowledge about yourself and enables you to improve.

Ego Army Troops deployed around your Rock of Fear		Ego Sentries Posted at lookout points around your Rock of Fear
• Negative inputs are deflected or converted into ones that are positive for the self.		• Negative inputs can be deflected, let in or disarmed. It's a choice.
• Negative inputs may generate an attack response.	Vs	• Positive inputs can be deflected, let in or disarmed. It's a choice.
• Positive inputs are let in.		• Limited army presence, so less likely to attack.
• Perception that there is no need to reflect on oneself or address beliefs or fears.		• Open to reflection and reappraising self-beliefs and fears.

The nature of the ego wrapping will depend on what is important to you, the scenario and the people who surround you; we generally have both armies and sentries. We may have sentries posted outside our

connectedness and **control** fears but a whole platoon deployed to defend our **competence** fear.

You will notice that I referred to the armies responding quickly but the sentries referring back to you to make a decision. This goes back to emotional vs cognitive responses. An ego response is a defensive and emotional response driven by our fears, which is why people with an Ego Army can have strong emotional responses (anger, shouting, tears). It is just the army on manoeuvres.

Seeing an army deployed creates fear in others. To protect themselves, they also deploy armies around their Rocks of Fear. The ego arms race continues until the organisation's environment becomes toxic, requiring employees to use all their resources just to protect themselves, leaving none for meaningful work.

If we are in an environment where we feel safe, spending fewer resources trying to hide or protect our fears by using sentries rather than armies, then we have more resources to think smartly and cognitively – which is what we pay our people for.

Leaders need to consider their ego wrapping and how it impacts the environment. Go back to the exercise we did at the beginning of this chapter: why you want/ wanted to be a leader. Here is the table redesigned.

Status	Salary	Validate your worth		Benefits	Authority	Expected of me	Be the boss
Perks	Grow self	Influence	Learn	Mentor	Autonomy	Support	Competition
Career	Prestige	Success	Coach	Do the fun stuff	Climb the corporate ladder	Connect	Recognition
Control	Serve	Legacy	Enable	Be in charge	Bigger car	Contribute	Gain higher peers
Grade	Power	Determine direction		Title	Delegate boring stuff		Promotion

You will have probably circled some words in black and some words in grey; those in black are more 'Ego' ('I') orientated than those in grey. The more words in black you circled, the more Ego Armies you may have deployed, but don't beat yourself up. It's OK to want status or nice things, as long as it's balanced with a recognition that your role as a leader is as much about others as it is about you. There is almost an expectation that leaders are ego driven. In his book *Why Do So Many Incompetent Men Become Leaders?* (which also acknowledges that there are incompetent female leaders), Tomas Chamorro-Premuzic unpacks how organisations' leader recruitment practices can result in those with strong egos being considered to have 'leadership qualities'.[127] Job descriptions ask for qualities such as 'entrepreneurial', 'proven track record', 'top performer' and even 'fearless', which evoke competitiveness and an organisation designed to play to egos. These are great qualities, but we often overuse our strengths when we are rewarded for them, and, in doing so, they become weaknesses.

Table 5: Strengths, when overused, can become weaknesses

Strength...	...when overused, can become...
Organised	Bossy/Controlling
Structured	Inflexible
Flexible	Unorganised/Unfocused
Strategic	Unrealistic or Impractical
Logical	Cold or lacking empathy

My friends often leave the organising of social events to me because I am a good organiser and I enjoy it. We decided to holiday together, and I organised it – brilliantly, if I may say so. But it turns out that having a minute-by-minute agenda for five days in a row doesn't make you organised, it makes you bossy. Who knew?

When considering the qualities you seek in your leaders, pay attention to the potential consequences of prized behaviours. An Ego Army may be too efficient, overusing a behavioural strategy that worked in the past. In my case, excellent organisation skills was a strategy that helped quiet my competence and **connectedness** fear: people were grateful and complimentary when I organised social events... until my army got too good at it! An organisation can determine whether its ethos has Ego Armies by observing its employees' emotional reactions and sense of safety. Employees will not feel safe if their leaders' egos lead to behaviour that only benefits themselves.

It may seem counterintuitive, but many high ego-ethos organisations are, or began as, family businesses. A family business is created to benefit the family and give them a better quality of life; however, the family firm can increase non-family employees' Rocks of Fear. Positions, particularly senior ones, are often allocated to family members, whether they are competent or not; thus, the non-family employee may feel that their **competence** is unacknowledged or irrelevant. Family members can also often behave as they wish, knowing they are unlikely to get sacked, while employees who are not family members don't have the security of family **connectedness** to eliminate that risk. Decisions are often made between family members in informal settings such as at the Sunday family BBQ, so employees may feel a lack of **control**. Often, if a non-family employee has a conflict with one family member, the whole family responds, making work life difficult; meanwhile, those who are 'in' with the family have greater safety than those who are not, compromising **connectedness**. Furthermore, the purpose of the company is to provide for the family, so there is a strong family ego ('us') focus rather than a **cause** that employees can buy into. As you can see, working for a family firm can feel very unsafe, and we haven't even begun to discuss the other mechanisms that help increase safety like mission, vision, policies, procedures, performance management and values that are often absent in family firms.

In any organisation, a dominant leadership style that is ego driven will lead to what I call a corporate shark tank. The culture becomes competitive, political, status orientated and 'macho' given the impermeable ego wrappings and hiding of vulnerabilities. This reduces safety for employees, which makes them harden their ego wrapping, further perpetuating the shark tank ethos.

For leaders to create an environment in which employees feel safe, the ethos must be created by those with impermeable egos who recognise that being a leader is not about them: there is no 'I' in leader.

The role of the leader is to ensure that employees perform. As we have seen, employees need plentiful resources and to feel safe in order to RISE; therefore, the leader needs to enable positive resources to enter the employee's balloon – not their own balloon. The true leader's balloon will rise vicariously through the rising of their team's balloon; their success will come from the success of others. This creates safety for employees: a feeling that their leader is invested in them and prioritises them over the leader's own needs. A boss, on the other hand, leaves their employees to fill their own balloons and focuses on only filling their own. As you can imagine, this creates a lack of safety among the employees.

Being a leader means losing the armies, or at least thinning them out. How do you do this? Well, it starts with knowing yourself.

Step 1: Reflect

When designing leadership programmes, alongside the modules about organisational behaviour, goal setting and structures, I always include a self-discovery module. It may be called 'Personal Effectiveness' or 'The Effective Leader' or 'You as a Leader', but it is all about knowing thyself. Many consider this 'the soft and fluffy' module, although I argue that if it is so 'soft and fluffy' why do you find it so hard? To effectively lead others, you need to understand yourself and why you behave the way you do:

- Why do you feel threatened by feedback?
- Why do you hate it when your team challenges you?
- Why does the thought of admitting you don't know make you feel uneasy?
- Why do you have to be in control?

Having read this book, we know that the answer to all of these questions is probably fear. But the leader needs to recognise *why* they respond the way they do, what the cause is. And this means reflecting. We talked about reflecting in the Flourish chapter and how it leads to learning; now I ask you to use it to learn about yourself. There are many reflection techniques out there, but here is a simple one that you can use anytime, anywhere:

1. Think about something to which you had an emotional response. You need not have shown your emotions, but you *felt* them.
2. Ask yourself why you felt like that.
3. Now ask 'Why?' again.

4. And again.

5. And again.

You need to repeat the Why questioning a minimum of five times to ensure that you get beyond the symptom and to the cause. Most people stop at the first Why and try to deal with it; keep asking until you get inside the Rock of Fear and understand what fear was being triggered.

In the example, most people would stop at the first Why and deal with the issue by going to the colleague and telling them that in future they need to ask the leader's permission. This treats the colleague like a child, reduces any possibility of innovation and dissuades challenge, depleting their resources and reducing psychological safety. But if you get to the root of the incident, it is not the colleague's problem; it is the leader's problem. The leader's fear was that they may be shown to be incompetent, and they were trying to maintain control.

It is possible to continue on the Whys: Why is it important that you feel competent? What do you fear will happen if you admit you do not know something, and why? Where does this fear come from? And now you are into 'Tell me about your childhood' territory, which is getting into counselling, not coaching, and you should avoid this unless you are a trained psychotherapist or you can refer the leader to one.

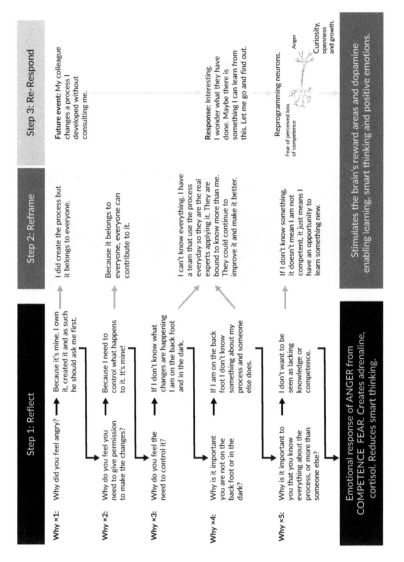

Step 1: Reflect

Why ×1: Why did you feel angry? → Because it's mine. I own it, created it and as such he should ask me first.

Why ×2: Why do you feel you need to give permission to make the changes? → Because I need to control what happens to it. It's mine!

Why ×3: Why do you feel the need to control it? → If I don't know what changes are happening I am on the back foot and in the dark.

Why ×4: Why is it important you are not on the back foot or in the dark? → If I am on the back foot I don't know something about my process and someone else does.

Why ×5: Why is it important to you that you know everything about the process, or more than someone else? → I don't want to be seen as lacking knowledge or competence.

Emotional response of ANGER from COMPETENCE FEAR. Creates adrenaline, cortisol. Reduces smart thinking.

Step 2: Reframe

I did create the process but it belongs to everyone.

Because it belongs to everyone, everyone can contribute to it.

I can't know everything. I have a team that use the process everyday so they are the real experts applying it. They are bound to know more than me. They could continue to improve it and make it better.

If I don't know something, it doesn't mean I am not competent, it just means I have an opportunity to learn something new.

Stimulates the brain's reward areas and dopamine enabling learning, smart thinking and positive emotions.

Step 3: Re-Respond

Future event: My colleague changes a process I developed without consulting me.

Response: Interesting. I wonder what they have done. Maybe there is something I can learn from this. Let me go and find out.

Reprogramming neurons.

Fear of perceived loss of competence

Anger

Curiosity, openness and growth.

The leader must reflect to understand why they reacted the way they did. Once they achieve this, the leader can progress to the next step in managing their Ego Army.

Step 2: Reframe

Here is where the growth mindset comes into its own. The example above shows a fixed mindset: there is right and wrong, mine and yours; knowledge is value, lack of knowledge is weak. Reframe this dialogue using a growth mindset.

Step 3: Re-respond

Reconsider how you would respond differently. This is the 'Abstract Conceptualisation' of Kolb's Learning Cycle discussed in the Flourish chapter. This will allow you to 'plan in your head' what you will do if the same thing happens again.

Consider the difference in feelings that Step 1 and Step 3 created. Step 1 created feelings that were negative psychological resources. In Step 3, the situation was the same but you created positive psychological resources. And, of course, the Step 3 response was better for the leader and their colleague's resources.

Ego-lite leaders

Being a leader with a lite ego does not disempower you or make you less able to make tough decisions or hold people to account for their performance. You still have all the responsibilities of being a leader, but in reducing the ego you will carry out your role in a way that creates a safe environment, enabling smart thinking, engagement and growth orientated employees. Consider the following questions to see if your leaders are ego-lite:

1. Are the leaders in your organisation aware of their strengths and development areas?

2. Are the leaders in your organisation comfortable asking for help from anyone, at any level in the organisation?

Ego-lite leaders have worked to understand themselves and like who they are. They don't feel the need to prove themselves as they are confident in their strengths and are aware of the areas they are continuing to develop. As such, they are not afraid to ask for help from anyone, at any level.

3. Do they refer to their team members in 'child-like' terms, such as 'the kids', or treat them like children?

Parents both nurture and control. When controlling, they tell children what to do. Leaders who tell people what to do are acting in a parental role, so they shouldn't be surprised when their employees act like children. The ego-lite leader asks, discusses and plans with others, adult to adult. As mentioned in Chapter 6, there are times when you have to tell, but most people will tolerate a small amount of instruction. If it is the only tool in your leadership toolbox, it will get old quickly.

4. When something goes wrong, do they look for 'the person responsible': someone to blame?

I don't think I have ever met anyone who goes to work to deliberately do a bad job. If people are not performing, it is because they are unable or unwilling to do the job. Whichever is the reason, the fault lies with their leader. When something unexpected happens, the enlightened leader is unafraid to ask what part they played in creating the issue – and then learns from it.

5. Do they interrupt others when speaking, or answer immediately afterwards?

We can't do two things at once. Multi-tasking is a myth; instead, we cognitively switch between single tasks rapidly, providing neither with our full attention. If you are already formulating your response to what someone is saying while they are saying it, then you are not listening – not properly, anyway. Doing so creates the impression that what you have to say is more important than what others are saying, an attitude which is driven by ego. Plus, it is rude. Keep doing it and others will eventually give up trying to say anything at all.

6. Do they really know their people?

To lead and motivate people, you need to understand them. Leaders should know what motivates each of their team members, what brings them to work, what's important to them, where they want to be, and what their passions and fears are. This intimacy helps with trust, but it requires you to spend time with your people, ask questions and listen.

7. Do they use a coaching leadership style?

We've talked about coaching in the Flourish chapter. Coaching does not need to be in the form of hour-long sessions; it can be 'in the moment' coaching. Whenever the leader wants an employee to do something, can they coach the employee through the activity instead of telling them how to do it?

8. Are they angry or emotionally volatile?

A primary cause of feeling unsafe is a lack of **consistency**. With an emotionally volatile leader, you never know whether you are going to get a happy leader or an angry leader. Do people have to walk on eggshells and choose their moments with this leader? If so, the

Ego Army is on high alert. This leader needs to work to understand themselves and reduce that ego.

9. Do they work long hours, being available 24/7?

This sets alarm bells ringing on so many levels. Firstly, it shows a lack of self-awareness: if the leader was self-aware, they would know they need rest, exercise, healthy food and downtime to perform effectively. It also suggests fear: fear of under-performing (**competence**), not keeping up with others (**connectedness**) or being seen by the organisation as a slacker (**cause, competence, control**). This behaviour can stem from a need to prove oneself. Secondly, it sets a precedent, creating an environment of fear for others who are unwilling or unable to work the same long hours. A culture of long hours puts the needs of the organisation above the basic needs of its employees, reducing safety.

10. Do they hold people to account?

If an employee is consistently under-performing, or is known throughout the organisation as a poor performer, this is because leaders have allowed it. The leader must hold people to account – assuming they have provided a strong arena. Fear can lead to poor performance management in organisations: leaders fear that they won't be liked (**connectedness**), that their efforts won't be successful (**competence**) or that the employee will respond emotionally (**control**).

A leader who is comfortable with themselves recognises that if any of these things happen, it does not affect who they are. The leader knows that managing performance is the right thing to do – for the individual, the team and the organisation – and that it is part of their job.

The culture and safety of employees depends on the leader. Research shows this is the primary predictor of employee safety.[128] A leader can maintain psychological safety for themselves and their employees if they manage performance with the intent to grow and not penalise; however, organisations can unwittingly and implicitly encourage employees to develop or maintain strong Ego Armies through their policies and processes.

Ego-lite processes and policies

Even if your organisation has the most ego-lite leaders, if processes and policies do not reflect this ethos, then alarm bells will ring. Employees will experience a lack of **consistency** in what is being said and how it is implemented. Processes and policies that support the employees' journey with your organisation need to reflect the ego-lite ethos. Using the Employee Lifecycle as a framework, here are some examples of how policies and processes can influence employees' perception of safety.

Attracting and recruiting

When recruiting employees to join your organisation (in particular, for leadership roles), what type of ego are you attracting? Job adverts for leaders include language that may attract ego-full leaders, encouraging behaviours that hint at Ego Armies. Those who have strong Ego Armies are often highly opinionated, not liking to be challenged but happy to challenge others. Job adverts with phrases such as 'top performer', 'expert' or 'proven track record' will attract individuals who meet these criteria; however, as it attracts those who appear to have high self-worth, some applicants will also have strong and well-trained Ego Armies.

As a side note, the fact that someone is a 'top performer' in their field does not automatically make them a good leader. I have seen many superb salespeople promoted into leadership roles, but the skills to be a top performing salesperson are not the same as to be an effective leader. Some of these salespeople turned out to be poor leaders; yet, because they had been good at selling, they remained in the leader role, creating untold psychological damage for the team.

Similarly, organisations look for competitive and (outwardly) confident employees, and both of these attributes are tools an Ego Army uses to protect its Rock of Fear. Job adverts ask for 'entrepreneurial' and 'success orientated' applicants, and once I even saw an advert for candidates who were 'fearless' – which we know from Chapter 3 is impossible!

These descriptors attract a particular type of leader: a leader that is focused on 'I', the type of leader who reduces psychological safety in the workplace. These job adverts could so easily be written to attract leaders who are focused on 'we' and would increase psychological safety in the people working for and with them.

If the interviewers are skilled, the recruitment process should filter out those sporting strong Ego Armies. Unskilled interviewers, such as those who use hypothetical questions (which have no correlation with what someone would actually do[129]) or who structure the interview like an informal chat, will be looking for people like themselves, thus perpetuating a culture or style. Even competency-based interviews compare candidates using the requirements in the job description, candidate A being more competitive, entrepreneurial and fearless than candidate B.

Onboarding

An organisation's onboarding process can provide the first clue about its levels of psychological safety. Note, onboarding is *not* an orientation programme. Orientation is transactional and concerns the support structures and 'need to know' information for all employees, such as health and safety and HR procedures. This is normally conducted by administration or HR. Onboarding gets the employee up to speed regarding performing their specific role; as such, it involves learning the job and performance objectives, coaching and leader involvement.

Not all organisations have formal onboarding. Many employ the 'in at the deep end' strategy, in which case new recruits should probably just walk away. If you don't get support at the beginning when the organisation knows you are new and need to learn, it's not likely the support will get any better over time.

Companies who provide onboarding programmes retain 91% of employees during the first year, and their employees were 69% more likely to remain at the company for up to three years.[130] If you think about it, starting a new job activates every fear you have: everything is new (**consistency**), you have left your old familiar team to join a new one (**connectedness**), you are taking on a new job (**competence**), and you don't know who to speak to or where to go to get things done (**control**). Hopefully, you will have researched the company before joining and will at least understand the **cause**, but you might want to understand more about how your role contributes to it. Employees need the onboarding process to create safety – perhaps more at this point than any time in the employment cycle.

Managing and rewarding performance

Appraisal is increasingly falling out of favour, given it is often poorly implemented. Once-a-year assessment of abilities (**competence**) provides little benefit to the employee. In fact, if it is related to pay or bonuses it may be harmful and can reduce psychological safety.

Reward practices in organisations can also induce fear. Commission creates a sword of Damocles that hangs over the employee, increasing fear and reducing resources. Bonus schemes are often based on the wider performance of the organisation or team, leaving the employee with little **control** over the outcome, and stopping previously received bonuses creates fear. Let's say a popular retailer pays its employees a bonus every year (**consistency**). In making the bonus annual, it ceases to be a bonus and becomes an expected payment. In 2008 the payment was 20% of a salesperson's salary, but in 2019 it was only 2%. Imagine that during these years you were doing the same job with equal competence, yet in 2019 you got 18% less. This wouldn't feel much like a reward – it would feel like punishment (**competence, control**).

Performance is usually measured as a product of output and goals achieved, both of which are important. However, it adds value to the outcome, rather than the process of achieving it (which is where much of the employee's learning took place). Thus, it is also important to reward growth, development, change and learning.

Development and growth

For organisations without a mindset of growth and a coaching leadership style that foster a learning ethos, training is used as both incentive – 'You can only attend this course if you reached a set standard' – or as punishment – 'You are not good enough, so go on this training course'. Either way, that creates a lack of safety. Employees need continuous development, making learning a **consistent**, and therefore a safe, activity.

Continuous development needs to span across a broad spectrum. Another reason for employees being promoted into leadership roles without the required skills may be that they followed a singular career development pathway. When working in IT, I met IT leaders who hated managing, preferring to code. This was apparent in their hands-off leadership-by-email style. When I asked why they had applied for the leader role, they responded that there were no alternative development paths. To progress their career, the only option was up: into leadership. Provide development options for those who wish to move into leadership and those who aim to progress within their specialty, and offer the same benefits, irrespective of which path is chosen. This will enable both employee career planning and organisational succession planning.

The succession planning itself can also provide an indicator of levels of safety. Who determined which employees are in the succession pipeline, and with what criteria? How transparent is the process? For those who want to be considered in the succession plans, are they aware of what they need to be developing to move to the next role? Is this planned and committed to? Does their leader enable it?

Exit

If you examine your exit interviews, I suspect that the majority of people left your organisation for 'career reasons'. For a learning organisation with multiple development paths, that reason should only account for a small percentage of leavers. Beware, though, that 'career reasons' is the stock phrase leavers use to mask the real reason: a poor leader. People join organisations; they leave leaders.

In summary, to improve psychological safety, employee performance and organisational performance, leaders need to be ego-lite with sentries not an army, focusing on the other person (the employee), and creating a feeling of positive intent and trust. Ego-lite leaders treat others like adults, acknowledging that they have their own thoughts, fears, concerns and skills. They hold these adults to account through coaching: asking questions and listening. Most importantly, ego-lite leaders are self-aware, brave enough to be vulnerable and having enough of a growth mindset to know that this is a good thing because it helps them learn about themselves and be a better leader.

QUESTIONS FOR YOUR ORGANISATION

- What mechanisms are in place for leaders to reflect and learn about themselves?
- What attributes are valued and rewarded in leaders? What consequences might arise from the overuse of these attributes?
- What vocabulary is used in your job adverts and job descriptions?
- How are new staff selected?
- Do you have an orientation programme or an onboarding programme for new starters? (You need both!) How do you support new starters?
- How are 'high potentials' identified? What makes them 'high potentials'? (Clue: it's not about current performance.)
- Why do people (really) leave your organisation?

Key learnings from this chapter

- We protect our fears using an Ego Army that is trained to deflect, disarm or attack perceived incoming threats.

- However, your army can be retrained or redeployed by increasing your self-awareness through reflection, reframing and responding.

- A weakness is an overused strength.

- As well as leaders, your policies and processes can impact employees' levels of psychological safety.

8

Psychological Safety: The Employee's Role

Let's say that as an organisation, you have developed leaders and processes that reduce employees' Rocks of Fear, enabling them to feel safe and deploy their psychological resources on flourishing. Well done! But something is not working: you still have employees that are in defensive mode, afraid and surviving, not thriving. A good leader will start by asking, 'What am I doing that is causing this person to behave like this?', but the employee also has a role to play in adding psychological resources to their own balloon.

Using the 'leading a horse to water' metaphor, organisations may provide the best trough on the market, containing the purest water, set in the perfect egolite arena. The organisation communicates about the quality of the water using story and providing purpose. Our horse may have even been trained on how to flourish by drinking from this nirvana-like trough or had 'drinking from this trough' set in its annual goals, with its leader measuring its development as much as its achievement. However, none of these initiatives will guarantee our equine friend will indulge. An organisation can provide all the mechanisms for resource maintenance and replenishment, but if an employee does not also take responsibility for their own resource levels, they will not have the same beneficial experiences as the SOUND employee.

Being SOUND helps you RISE

My other book, *RISE,* provides extensive tools and techniques to help individuals maintain their own resource levels, but this chapter will provide a summary of the employee's role in being resource-full.

Every employee, at every level of the organisation, has a role to play in their own psychological, emotional and physical well-being – in contributing positive resources to their balloon. Expecting others to do this for you shows a passive approach to your well-being. It makes you a victim of circumstances and situations.

Although people with this mindset will not recognise it, being a victim is a choice. Victims often have heavy Rocks of Fear and are the passive aggressive version of bullies. They have Ego Armies that use a strategy of defence rather than attack, but the consequences can be as damaging as the bully's attack strategy: it creates fear in others. Those who work with the victim know that the victim has their own self-interest at heart and will be quick to protect themselves from blame and shift responsibility wherever possible. The victim chooses to dismiss organisational and leader stories with negativity and cynicism. They flourish in environments where their arena has not been clearly identified because then nothing is their responsibility. They choose not to flourish (this might expose their **competence**), and although they will claim not to have an ego they have an Ego Army skilled in the art of tactical defence and outmanoeuvring others. It's a comfortable place to be; having no responsibility or accountability and being paid for it. This person is your organisation's dead weight, and it's even worse if they're a leader in your organisation.

Having a boss who is a victim is disempowering and frustrating. Victim leaders use phrases such as, 'I would give you the pay rise, but it's not up to me, it's head office' or 'I don't agree with it but I'm just doing what I am told'. These statements may be accurate, but as a leader you are expected to be the 'face' of the organisation and thus show consensus. And consensus does not mean agreement. Consensus is about a group agreeing a common approach, even if you don't agree with it. You have voiced your concerns, expressed disagreement, but ultimately you agree that whatever the final decision, you will implement it as if you agreed with it. That's what leaders do. Victim leaders will not fight the employee's corner or the organisations, they will not sing anyone's praises and the only person they will keep SAFE is themselves.

Employees may have legitimate reasons for feeling like a victim. If they do not feel safe and their resources are depleted their leader needs to address this. But meanwhile, the employee (leader or not) also needs to work to change their own mindset. It is reciprocal – *both* parties need to contribute to the balloon.

Based on my research, I teach people that to help create sound mental well-being and develop sound thinking, they need to be resource-full. This chapter will provide a synopsis of what makes a SOUND individual.

Sustain self

Employees need to sustain themselves with the basic physiological resources the body needs. This may be boring, but it's true. We all need rest; even machines have to switch off. Employees need to manage their working hours and learn to say no, take breaks, use all their holiday entitlement, switch off and, if ill, go home and get better. They should also get eight hours of sleep – every night – and eat well. The brain uses up to 25% of our energy *at rest*, so they need to provide it with quality fuel: fruit, vegetables, water, and regular healthy meals. Exercise strengthens the body and mind, so employees should make time for it.

Omnipurpose

Just as organisations need clear purposes, individuals need to understand theirs. Are they living authentic lives? Research has shown that employees who are doing a job they dislike or that goes against their personal values are more prone to depression, poor self-esteem and poorer well-being.[131] Living and working according to your values and purpose increases engagement, job satisfaction and performance.[132] From a psychological perspective, those working in an environment that aligned with their personal values showed reduced cortisol production in response to stressors: they were better able to deal with stress.[133]

A discrepancy between the person you are and who you have to be at work can lead to feelings of dejection, shame, embarrassment and even feeling threatened.[134] Not only is the individual deploying valuable psychological resources in being someone they are not, but the resulting emotions create negative resources.

Employees need self-awareness to understand their truth, who they are, what they value and their purpose. And then they need to live according to this self-knowledge.

Useful narrative

One of the most powerful realisations I have ever had was that I don't have to believe everything my brain tells me. As mentioned in Chapter 1, emotions are merely messages from our brain telling us that we *may* want to respond in a particular way. Sometimes the messages are a bit over-zealous and sometimes they are simply wrong. Our internal narrative can disseminate self-doubt, insecurity and fear, and it can lie – or at least misinterpret or exaggerate. Being aware of the internal narrative and understanding it can help us manage how we deal with life. It lets us select the resources that we put into our balloon and those which would serve us better if we reframed them or let them go altogether. We choose where we focus our attention.

Being open to the unique and new drives us to explore and broadens our knowledge and experiences. This increases our ability to deal with the unexpected, reducing our **control**, **consistency** and **competence** fears. Openness allows us to develop different thought patterns, becoming more creative and developing new options. From a physiological perspective, it helps exercise and build new neurons in the brain. Being open to the new is essential for adaptation and growth.

Discernment

We always have options in life. Even when it comes to death, we are increasingly able to choose how and when this happens. You may not like the look of option B, but at least it is an option. You choose how you live your life, what you believe and where you focus your attention. Being discerning about what we allow into our balloon can increase our sense of **control** and **competence**. True, there are things in life we cannot do anything about – Covid-19 being one example – but we can choose how to deal with them.

Applying discernment doesn't always banish fear, but the brain will respond to what you focus on, adjusting the amount of cortisol, adrenaline, dopamine and serotonin you produce accordingly. This, in turn, impacts the way you process information and your levels of resilience. Choosing where your attention goes and selecting your responses are key to enabling your balloon to RISE.

Luckily, everyone can learn to apply the tools to become SOUND. There are many ways to achieve SOUNDness; however, as we saw in Chapter 2, an employee needs the psychological resources to ensure they are in a dopamine-serotonin state before they can learn new techniques. The organisation therefore must ensure that they are not depleting employees' psychological resources.

Teach SOUND skills incrementally, so they only require a few resources at a time to learn. As the employee learns each skill, their positive resources increase and their balloon starts to RISE – which means the leader's balloon begins to RISE and so does your organisation.

Conclusion: Up, Up And Away

There we have it. Organisational performance is all about hot-air balloons, rocks, armies and, of course, leaders. In exploring psychological resources, we have taken a journey into the brain and how it functions. There is still a lot to learn about the brain, but we know more about it now than when many of the popular management models being implemented in organisations were designed. With this new knowledge, perhaps we should plan how we interact with employees in a way that compliments how the brain works, rather than contradicting it.

We have learned that brain inputs can increase our capacity for logical and reasoned thought, learning and innovating. What goes into the brain can also deplete our psychological capacity, leading to defensive responses and narrow thinking. Given that we spend much of our time at work, the working environment provides many of these resources: both positive and negative. Luckily, individuals, leaders and organisations each have some control over this.

Although learning about cognitive resources provides great insight, it does mean the role of the leader is becoming more complex, nuanced and psychological. There are so many people in leadership roles who are psychologically unprepared or unskilled, and this has an indirect cost for organisations. My research showed that there have been many attempts to quantify this cost, and, while I found no consistent answer, the common thread across all the attempts to measure the cost was that it is significant. When you consider the drop in employee performance from poor workplace experiences, toxic culture, poor change management, lack of support and the consequent lack of engagement, the cost adds up. This means that those organisations who are able to create a SAFE environment will retain their talent – and it is this talent that will distinguish your business from the competition.

Leadership is not a position; it is as much a skilled profession as engineering, architecture and medicine. There are organisations that try to enforce this thinking, such as the Institute of Leadership and Management, the Chartered Institute of Personnel and Development and the Chartered Management

Institute in the UK. However, there still seems to be a belief that leadership is something that anyone can pick up. People attempt to all the time, but how much damage do they cause during the years of learning to be self-aware, reducing egos and understanding their impact on others?

Leadership starts with a leader creating their own balloon, reducing their own Rock of Fear, understanding their own truth and thriving. All of these things can be taught, and they often have to be. When teaching leaders, I often hear, 'I wish someone had told me this years ago', and that is why I am also creating a RISE book for individuals like your employees (and you!). Leadership skills are life skills, and today there is no excuse for poor leadership. Science has given us the knowledge to lead and get the most out of our employees. This book has taken you through the steps to apply that knowledge to create SAFE environments and SOUND employees.

Glossary

Adrenaline   Adrenaline (also known as epinephrine) and noradrenaline (also known as norepinephrine) are two related hormones that are produced in the adrenal glands (situated near the kidneys). They prepare the body for 'fight or flight' in times of stress, causing increased heart rate, heightened blood pressure, sweating and feeling shaky.

Allostasis   The process that the brain uses to keep balance between stresses and coping.

Alpha waves   Brain waves that operate at 8–12 Hz and occur when you are feeling relaxed.

Amygdala   The part of the brain that is responsible for noticing and processing fear.

Appetite motivational system A phrase coined by Masterson and Crawford (1982) to differentiate different sources of motivation. The appetite motivational system is goal directed behaviour towards gain.

Approach vs avoid The messages that your brain sends you in the form of emotions will tell you to approach (perception of safety) or to avoid (perception of threat).

Beta waves Brain waves that operate at 12–35 Hz and occur when you are concentrating and problem solving.

Binary thinking When you see the world in two dimensions: things are either good or bad, right or wrong.

Brain waves The electrical voltages at which the brain operates.

Cognitive processes The mental processes in the brain: thinking, knowing, perceiving, memory, reasoning, etc.

Cognitive resources See Resources

Cortisol A hormone triggered in response to threat.

Covid-19   A virus that at the time of writing has no known cure and thus forces us all to work from home and learn to use Zoom.

Defensive motivational system   A phrase coined by Masterson and Crawford (1982) to differentiate different sources of motivation. The defensive motivational system is 'away' from behaviour driven by fear of a perceived threat.

Delta waves   Brain waves that operate at 0.5–4 Hz and occur when you are in deep sleep.

Discernment   Being choosy; in this book's context, about what resources you allow into your balloon.

Dopamine   A neurotransmitter that comes into play when experiencing reward/pleasure. It is also the main type of transmitter in the frontal cortex and helps control smart thinking.

Ego Army   The protection that sits around our Rock of Fear. It may attack when your fears are activated or your comfort is threatened.

Emotions   Also known as 'feelings'. These are messages that the brain sends you. The messages may or may not be correct.

Equilibrium That happy state when you have enough resources to be able to deal with whatever life is throwing at you.

Evolve To grow, to change, to adapt to the environment. Essential for long-term mental well-being.

Exploit Extracting the most from the existing and known.

Explore The action to seek the new or novel.

Fight flight freeze The brain's automatic response to threat, triggered by the amygdala.

Frontal cortex The front part of the brain that is responsible for clever and advanced thinking.

Gamma waves Brain waves that operate at >35 Hz and occur when you are excited and highly alert.

Growth mindset A concept from Carol Dweck that reframes thinking so that experiences become a learning opportunity, allowing one to grow and improve.

Hippocampus The part of the brain involved in emotions, learning and memories.

Imposter syndrome   A self-belief that you are not as competent or capable as others believe you to be.

Initiative   The principle of being creative, proactive and applying smart thinking to new situations.

Limbic system   A term used to refer to the multiple parts of the brain that control our emotional responses.

Myelin   The fatty insulation that surrounds a neuron.

Narrative   The story you tell yourself. Sometimes it's fiction; sometimes it's not. Can be useful or not.

Neuron   A nerve cell in the brain that transmits information in the form of electrical impulses.

Neuronal path   A group of connected neurons linking multiple parts of the brain together.

Optimism   A belief that good things will happen.

Peripheral processing   Processing information and events using the emotional/limbic system.

Psychological safety   Defined by William Kahn in 1990 as being able to engage oneself fully into the workplace without fear of negative consequences to the self or career. This was later adapted to being able AND willing by S Mather (2020).

Reflection Looking back over events and learning about yourself from them.

Reframe To position a thought or view in another way to reduce its negative impact.

Resilience Having sufficient resources to deal with life's challenges. Similar to Equilibrium.

Resources (Cognitive) 'Stuff' that goes into your brain: information, thoughts, social media. They can be helpful or unhelpful.

Return vs Learn A decision to be made when returning from a loss of equilibrium as to whether to continue as before or learn from the experience.

RISE What you will do when your balloon is full of helpful resources: be **R**esilient, have **I**nitiative, **S**witch thinking and **E**volve.

Rock of Fear The combinations of fears that may weigh down your balloon and sap your resources.

Self-Efficacy Term originally coined by psychologist Albert Bandura. It refers to our belief and perception of our own capabilities. This may or may not bear resemblance to actual capabilities.

Serotonin   A neurotransmitter that stimulates 'feel good' hormones.

Shift   The ability to see things from a different view and change opinions; to respond in a different way.

SOUND   Mnemonic for an employee who has created the cognitive resources to RISE by: **S**ustaining the brain, identifying their **O**mnipurpose, creating a **U**seful **N**arrative and being **D**iscerning as to where they focus their attention.

Stress   The response to pressure on our resources.

Sustenance   Nutrients and behaviours that 'feed' our body and brain.

Synapse   A connection between two neurons where a chemical process takes place.

Systemic or central processing   Processing of events or situations using the smart part of the brain.

Theta   Brain waves that operate at 4–8 Hz and occur when you are in a state of reduced consciousness but not asleep. These can lead to bursts of gamma waves when you hit upon a brilliant idea or solution.

VUCA A military term used to describe Volatile, Uncertain, Complex and Ambiguous environments. Now adopted by organisations to describe current markets and operating environments.

Appendices

Appendix 1: How psychologically safe do your employees feel?

Rate the following statements in terms of how often you believe they occur: rarely, sometimes or often. Note: psychological safety can vary across areas of the organisation, so consider answering with a specific team, function or department in mind.

Score your answer using this guide:

For Questions 1–10	Rarely	Sometimes	Often
	2	1	0

For Questions 11–20	Rarely	Sometimes	Often
	0	1	2

	Rarely	Sometimes	Often	Score
1. Emails have a plethora of cc's on them				
2. The bcc function on emails is used				
3. Employee surveys have to be anonymous				
4. There is a strong union or employee representative body				
5. There are high absence rates due to stress or mental health issues				
6. The major reason for leaving the organisation is 'career'				
7. Learning and Development is the role of the HR/Talent Development team				
8. There is a dominant style or personality type at the leadership level				
9. It is a struggle to get things done, particularly to implement change, due to passive aggressive behaviours				
10. Employees are implicitly expected to work long hours and/ or be available after hours				

	Rarely	Sometimes	Often	Score
11. Coaching is prevalent within the organisation				
12. There is always a lot of discussion and debate in meetings				
13. Employees have friends at work who they see outside of work				
14. Employees tell their leaders about any personal problems they are having				
15. Employees are rewarded for their learning and development				
16. There is noticeable employee diversity at all levels of the organisation, particularly at leadership level				
17. Social events (BBQs, Christmas parties, etc.) are well attended across all levels of the organisation				
18. Leaders are continuously developing and improving their leadership skills				
19. Some of our best ideas and innovations come from employees' voluntary suggestions				
20. Every employee sees their manager (physically or virtually) on a one-to-one basis at least once a month				

Add the scores in the right-most column of the question sheet. When complete, total up your score.

Your score was between
0 and 10
There are sufficient indicators to suggest a low level of psychological safety within your organisation. Given the wide range of lower-scoring statements, your organisation may need to address this systemically.

Your score was between
11 and 30
There are some indicators to suggest a low level of psychological safety for some activities. It may be worth focusing on these to understand why.

Your score was between
31 and 40
Your answers suggest that your employees feel psychologically safe. You should be able to see this in the form of collaboration, innovation and performance. Well done.

Appendix 2: Growth mindset questionnaire

Think about each of these statements. Focus on your emotions. Mark the response (A or B) that best describes your emotional response:

1. You are in a meeting and several people are discussing something you know nothing about.

   A) *I have no idea what they are on about. I hope they don't find out.*

   B) *No idea what they are talking about, I'll ask them to fill me in.*

2. Your company is restructuring. They don't have a role for you in your specialism. They can offer you a role in another part of the business where you have never worked before.

   A) *I am a {insert your job function here}. It's what I do and who I am. I can't/won't do this new job.*

   B) *OK, this is new, bit concerned but I could learn a lot. I might like it.*

3. One of your team members has just upset a customer, so much so that the customer has threatened to leave/cancel an order.

   A) *I am furious. That team member needs to be dealt with.*

   B) *Wow, I wonder what happened.*

4. You have messed up.

   A) *Uh oh. How can I cover this up before anyone finds out?*

   B) *I'll tell my boss what I have done and how I am going to fix it.*

5. A colleague who started with your company at the same time as you has been promoted.

   A) *Who did they sleep with?*

   B) *Good on them. I wonder what I can learn from them.*

6. An initiative you were leading has hit a setback: the senior stakeholder has changed and they are going to take some persuading.

   A) *Drat. My logic has worked once, if it doesn't work this time, there is no point arguing with idiots, I'll move on.*

   B) *My argument is not working with this person. What do I need to do differently?*

7. Your boss has given you some negative feedback that you disagree with.

   A) *S/He is an idiot. What do they know?*

   B) *Really, interesting perspective. Tell me more.*

8. Your boss sees you are tired, you have been working hard. They suggest you go home early and take a long weekend.

A) *No way, this is a trick and will be held against me. Must not show weakness.*

B) *They are right, that's a good idea.*

9. It takes a lot of effort for one of your team to complete a task.

A) *Give the task to someone who can do it more easily. Play to strengths.*

B) *How can I help this person?*

10. You have been asked to take on a new project, something you have never done before.

A) *Why are they doing this? I can't do this. Why are they setting me up to fail?*

B) *OK, interesting. No idea where to start. I'll get some help.*

For the above questions, score 1 point for each 'B' answer, then add up the total points. Where does your score come on the continuum below?

	Mainly fixed mindset			Mixed				Mainly growth mindset		
Score:	0	1	2	3	4	5	6	7	8	9	10

Many of you will have answered 'B' to several of the questions, giving you a high score. After all, these are the socially 'preferred' answers. But deep down you will know some of your responses are really the 'A' ones. That's OK. We all have some elements of a fixed mindset. Go back to the questions that you secretly know are more 'A' and consider what your answers may say about how you view various aspects of your life.

Each of the ten questions relates to a different area and strength. Using your score, take a look at the following table to see what it might say about your mindset. Do you agree or disagree?

Q.	Views About...	Mainly Fixed Mindset	Mixed	Mainly Growth Mindset
1 ___ 2	The World	Unchangeable: find out who you are and your place in the world.	There are some areas in life that you can affect, but others are predetermined and no amount of effort will change them.	Changing: life is about deciding who and what you want to be and developing the skills and abilities to achieve it.
3 ___ 4	Mistakes	Hides or ignores mistakes.	We all make mistakes and they can be corrected.	Sees mistakes as a learning opportunity. Not always about right or wrong.

Continued

Cont.

Q.	Views About...	Mainly Fixed Mindset	Mixed	Mainly Growth Mindset
5	Success of Others	Feels threatened: compares self with others; competition highlights deficits.	Selects arena of competition: will only play if they are convinced they will win or it makes them look good.	Looks for people to learn from: competition can improve everyone.
6	Difficulty / Obstacles	Gives up.	As long as there is progress, will continue.	Keeps going because it will teach them something.
7	Feedback & Criticism	Ignores feedback; sees as a list of their faults.	Feedback can be good as long as it's relevant.	Requests both complimentary and critical feedback: it's a way to grow.
8	Offers of Help	Refuses help: it's a sign of weakness or incompetence.	Accepts help when offered.	Seeks out help: it can improve outcomes.
9	Effort	If I have to put this much effort in, I'm not very good.	Effort is a necessary evil. Prefers things to be easier and simple.	Effort is a path to mastery.

Continued

Cont.

Q.	Views About...	Mainly Fixed Mindset	Mixed	Mainly Growth Mindset
10	Challenge	Potential threats.	Will take on clear, immediate goals that are in areas in which they already feel confident.	Embraces challenges, even when they can't see the 'how'.

Once you're aware of your views, consider how you might begin to change one area. Reflect on a past incident when you responded with a fixed mindset. How did that feel? Then, replay the incident with a growth mindset as suggested in the table above. How does that feel? It is likely to feel better, which means that if it's not adding to your resources at least it's depleting them less.

Notes

1. Asongu, Financial Sector Competition and Knowledge Economy; Baard et al., Performance Adaptation; Haskel & Martin, Technology, wages, and skill shortages; Truce, Knowledge economy in financial services

2. Bennett & Lemoine, What a difference a word makes

3. Cartwright, New forms of work organization; Schuler et al., Global talent management, p10

4. Weick & Quinn, Organizational change and development

5. McArthur, Beating VUCA's Whiplash Factor

6. Ployhart & Bliese, I-ADAPT theory

7. Cambridge Dictionary, https://dictionary. cambridge.org/dictionary/english/sound

8. Masten et al., Resilience and development, p426

9. Bonanno, Loss, trauma, and human resilience; Glantz & Sloboda, Analysis and Reconceptualization of Resilience; Luthar et al., The Construct of Resilience; McEwen, In pursuit of resilience; Staudinger et al., Reserve Capacity in Later Adulthood; Wagnild & Young, Resilience Scale; Petty & Briñol, Emotion and persuasion; Cacioppo et al., The neuroscience of persuasion

10. Wheeler et al., Resistance to persuasion as self-regulation; Maslach, Burnout, p5; Atouba & Lammers, Burnout among IT professionals; Maslach et al., Job burnout

11. Maslach et al., Job burnout; Aspinwall et al., Understanding how optimism works; Baumeister et al., The strength model of self-control

12. Carver, Scheier & Segerstrom, Optimism; Luthans & Youssef, Emerging positive organizational behavior; Peterson, The future of optimism; Seligman & Steen, Positive Psychology Progress: Empirical Validation of Interventions

13. Marois & Ivanoff, Information Processing in the Brain

14. Hackman & Oldham, Motivation through the Design of Work

15. Britt et al., Employee Resilience; Gordon & Coscarelli, Recognizing and fostering resilience; Kumpfer, Factors and processes contributing to resilience; Meredith et al., Resilience in the U.S. Military, p2; Park, Implications of posttraumatic growth for individuals; Ryff & Singer, Flourishing under fire; Sommer, Keeping Positive and Building Strength; Sutcliffe & Vogus, Organizing for resilience

16. Baumeister et al., Ego depletion; Muraven & Baumeister, Self-regulation and depletion of limited resources; Muraven et al., Conserving Self-Control Strength, 13

17. Job et al., Ego depletion

18. Francis & Job, Lay theories of willpower

19. Baumeister et al., Personal accounts of changes in self-esteem; Hobfoll, Social and psychological resources and adaptation; Holahan et al., Resource loss, resource gain, and depressive symptoms; Keinan et al., Suppression of erroneous competing responses; King et al., Posttraumatic stress disorder in Vietnam veterans; Norris & Kaniasty, Social support in times of stress

20. McEwen, Plasticity of the Hippocampus; McEwen, In pursuit of resilience

21. Arnsten et al., The effects of stress exposure on prefrontal cortex, 10; Compas, Psychobiological processes of stress and coping; Kalisch et al., Deconstructing and reconstructing resilience; McEwen & Sapolsky, Stress and Cognitive Function

22. See Note 7 for this chapter

23. McEwen & Gianaros, The brain in stress and adaptation

24. McEwen, In pursuit of resilience

25. Hobfoll, Social and psychological resources and adaptation; Hobfoll, Conservation of Resources, p516

26. Hobfoll, Social and psychological resources and adaptation; Seligman & Csikszentmihalyi, Positive psychology

27. Albarracín & Kumkale, Affect as information in persuasion; Schwarz & Clore, Judgments of well-being

28. Bohner et al., Information Processing Approaches to Persuasion; Petty & Briñol, Emotion and persuasion; Sweldens et al., Awareness in Attitude Formation

29. Gawronski & Bodenhausen, Associative and propositional processes in evaluation

30. Bohner, G., Erb, H.-P., & Siebler, F. (2008).
Information Processing Approaches to
Persuasion: Integrating Assumptions from
the Dual- and Single-Processing Perspectives.
In W. D. Crano & R. Prislin (Eds.), *Attitudes
and attitude change* (pp161-189). New York:
Taylor and Francis. 4. Petty, R. E., & Briñol,
P. (2015). Emotion and persuasion: Cognitive
and meta-cognitive processes impact attitudes.
Cognition and Emotion, 29(1), 1-26. doi:
10.1080/02699931.2014.967183 5. Sweldens,
S., Corneille, O., & Yzerbyt, V. (2014). The
Role of Awareness in Attitude Formation
Through Evaluative Conditioning. *Personality
and Social Psychology Review*, 18(2), 187-209.
doi:10.1177/1088868314527832

31. Petty & Briñol, Emotion and persuasion

32. Cacioppo et al., The neuroscience of persuasion;
Mather, Employee Safety; Wheeler et al.,
Resistance to persuasion as self-regulation

33. Kumpfer, Factors and processes contributing to
resilience, p180

34. Bonanno, Loss, trauma, and human resilience;
Zautra & Reich, Resilience, p173; Garmezy,
Resilience in Children's Adaptation; Masten,
Ordinary magic

35. Bonanno, Loss, trauma, and human resilience;
Masten, Ordinary magic; Glantz & Sloboda,
Analysis and Reconceptualization of Resilience;

Luthar et al., The Construct of Resilience; McEwen, In pursuit of resilience; Staudinger et al., Resilience in Later Adulthood; Wagnild & Young, Resilience Scale

36. Gordon, Resilient African American High School Students; Luthans, Positive organizational behavior

37. Youssef & Luthans, Positive organizational behavior in the workplace; Beltman et al., Thriving not just surviving, p186; Näswall et al., EmpRes Measurement Properties, p1; Compas, Psychobiological processes of stress and coping, p226

38. Joseph et al., Changes in outlook following disaster; Tedeschi & Calhoun, The Posttraumatic Growth Inventory; Tedeschi & Calhoun, Posttraumatic Growth

39. Bensimon, Trauma, PTSD and posttraumatic growth; Frazier et al., Self-Reported Posttraumatic Growth; Videka-Sherman & Lieberman, The limits of recovery

40. Park, Posttraumatic growth for individuals

41. Pargament & Park, Merely a Defense?

42. Joseph et al., Changes in outlook following disaster

43. Tedeschi & Calhoun, Posttraumatic Growth; Wortman, Posttraumatic Growth

44. Bensimon, Trauma, PTSD and posttraumatic growth; Wortman, Posttraumatic Growth; Bonanno et al., Trajectories of grieving, pp287, 307; Helgeson et al., Benefit finding and growth

45. Egeland et al., Resilience as Process

46. Zautra & Reich, Resilience, p173; Lang, The Emotion Probe; Lazarus & Folkman, Emotions and coping

47. Albarracín & Kumkale, Affect as information in persuasion; Clore & Huntsinger, How emotions inform judgment and regulate thought; Huntsinger et al., The affective control of thought

48. Zautra & Reich, Resilience, p173; Tedeschi & Calhoun, Posttraumatic Growth; Cacioppo et al., The affect system; Lang, The Emotion Probe; Richardson, The metatheory of resilience and resiliency

49. Bonanno, Resilience in the face of potential trauma; Caza & Milton, Resilience at work

50. Kumpfer, Factors and processes contributing to resilience, p180; Park, Implications of posttraumatic growth for individuals; Britt et al., Employee Resilience; Gordon & Coscarelli, Recognizing and fostering resilience; Meredith et al., Resilience in the U.S. Military, p2; Ryff & Singer, Flourishing under fire; Sommer, Keeping Positive and Building Strength; Sutcliffe & Vogus, Organizing for resilience

51. Bennett & Lemoine, What VUCA really means for you, p27

52. Chan, Understanding Adaptation to Changes in the Work Environment

53. Cousins, Design thinking; De Meuse, Learning agility

54. Rogers et al., Effects of life-event stress and hardiness on peripheral vision

55. Gulotta et al., Attentional capture of irrelevant sound input in adolescents

56. Girotti et al., Prefrontal cortex executive processes affected by stress

57. Hohnen & Murphy, The optimum context for learning; Willis, The current impact of neuroscience on teaching and learning

58. Albarracín & Kumkale, Affect as information in persuasion; Clore & Huntsinger, How emotions inform judgment and regulate thought; Huntsinger et al., The affective control of thought

59. Clore & Huntsinger, How emotions inform judgment and regulate thought; Bodenhausen et al., Happiness and stereotypic thinking in social judgment; Isbell et al., The role of affect; Isen et al., Positive affect facilitates creative problem solving

60. Kaplan & Norton, *The Balanced Scorecard*

61. Johnson, S. (1999). *Who Moved My Cheese?*

62. Beechler & Woodward, The global 'war for talent'; Weick & Quinn, Organizational change and development; Worrall & Cooper, *Quality of Working Life 2012*

63. Beechler & Woodward, The global 'war for talent'; McArthur, Beating VUCA's Whiplash Factor

64. Atouba & Lammers, Examining the relationships between participative organisational communication practices and burnout among IT professionals; Maslach, *Burnout: The Cost of Caring*

65. Alegre et al., The real mission of the mission statement; Bowen, Mission and Vision; Hurth et al., Organisational purpose, 67

66. Jensen et al., Optimism and employee performance in the banking industry; Tuten & Neidermeyer, Performance, satisfaction and turnover in call centers

67. Carver et al., How Coping Mediates the Effect of Optimism on Distress; Klein & Helweg-Larsen, Perceived Control and the Optimistic Bias; McKenna, It won't happen to me; Scheier et al., Coping with stress

68. Hurth et al., Organisational purpose, 67; Hackman & Oldham, Motivation through Design of Work

69. Baldoni, Purpose Is What Your Organization Needs Most; Baumeister & Vohs, The pursuit of meaningfulness in life; Quinn & Thankor, Creating a Purpose-Driven Organization

70. Auvinen et al., Constructing leadership by storytelling; Harris & Barnes, Leadership storytelling

71. Denning, Effective storytelling; Auvinen et al., Constructing leadership by storytelling

72. Hovland et al., Assimilation and contrast effects

73. Peters, Get Innovative or Get Dead; Ciulla, The state of leadership ethics

74. Ready, How storytelling builds next-generation leaders, 63

75. Auvinen et al., Constructing leadership by storytelling

76. Denning, Effective storytelling

77. Rich, On the streets

78. Small et al., Sympathy and callousness

79. Sinek, 'How great leaders inspire action' (2009), www.ted.com/talks/simon_sinek_how_great_leaders_inspire_action, accessed February 2021

80. Direnzo & Greenhaus, Job Search and Voluntary Turnover

81. Faraj & Yan, Boundary work in knowledge teams; Gibson & Gibbs, Unpacking the Concept of Virtuality

82. Faraj & Yan, Boundary work in knowledge teams; Gibson & Gibbs, Unpacking the Concept of Virtuality; Cartwright, New forms of work organization; Edmondson & Harvey, Cross-boundary teaming for innovation; Heerwagen et al., The Changing Nature of Organizations, Work, and Workplace

83. De Smet et al., Organizing for the future, p3; Cartwright, New forms of work organization; Buhler, Changing organizational structures; McArthur, Beating VUCA's Whiplash Factor; Mohrman, Geographically dispersed teams and networks, 63

84. Sharkie, Precariousness under the new psychological contract; De Witte et al., The association between job insecurity and health and well-being; Guest, Human resource management and employee well-being

85. Faraj & Yan, Boundary work in knowledge teams; McNeil et al., Interprofessional practice and professional identity threat

86. Faraj & Yan, Boundary work in knowledge teams; McNeil et al., Interprofessional practice and professional identity threat

87. www.dictionary.com, accessed February 2021

88. Faraj & Yan, Boundary work in knowledge teams; Carmeli & Gittell, High-quality relationships; Simpson, Psychological foundations of trust

89. Locke & Latham, New directions in goal-setting theory

90. Locke & Latham, New directions in goal-setting theory, p265

91. Stajkovic & Luthans, Social cognitive theory and self-efficacy; Thompson et al., Stretch targets

92. Bandura, Fearful expectations and avoidant actions; Wood & Bandura, Impact of Conceptions of Ability

93. Locke & Latham, Work motivation and satisfaction

94. Garland, Task Goals and Human Performance

95. Eden & Ravid, Pygmalion Versus Self-Expectancy; Mather, Employee Safety

96. Scheier & Carver, Optimism, Coping, and Health, p219

97. Cozzarelli, Coping with abortion; Peterson, The future of optimism; Segerstrom et al., Optimism is associated with mood; Seligman, *Learned optimism*; Snyder et al., Optimism and hope constructs; Carver & Scheier, Positive and Negative Affect

98. Youssef & Luthans, Positive organizational behavior in the workplace, p778

99. Stajkovic & Luthans, Social cognitive theory and self-efficacy; Bandura, Fearful expectations and avoidant actions; Bandura, *Self-efficacy: The exercise of control*

100. Eden & Ravid, Pygmalion Versus Self-Expectancy

101. Locke & Latham, Work motivation and satisfaction

102. Wood & Bandura, Impact of Conceptions of Ability; Bandura & Wood, Effect of Perceived Controllability; Wood et al., Mechanisms governing organizational performance

103. Li & Bagger, Role ambiguity and self-efficacy; Schabracq & Cooper, The changing nature of work and stress; Pulakos, Performance Management Can Be Fixed

104. Thoits, Stressors and problem-solving; Werner, Risk, Resilience, and Recovery; Rini et al., Psychological adaptation and birth outcomes; Rutter, Psychosocial resilience and protective mechanisms

105. Stajkovic & Luthans, Social cognitive theory and self-efficacy; Wood et al., Mechanisms governing organizational performance; Bandura & Locke, Negative self-efficacy and goal effects revisited; Cervone, Goal setting and

self-regulatory processes; Tierney & Farmer,
Creative self-efficacy

106. Thompson & Gomez, The Role of Self-Esteem
and Self-Efficacy

107. Bandura, A. (1982). Self-Efficacy Mechanism in
Human Agency. *American Psychologist, 37*(2),
p140. doi: 10.1037/0003-066x.37.2.122

108. Fink, A., Koschutnig, K., Benedek, M., Reishofer,
G., Ischebeck, A., Weiss, E. M. and Ebner, F.
(2012), Stimulating creativity via the exposure
to other people's ideas. *Hum. Brain Mapp.*, 33:
2603–2610. https://doi.org/10.1002/hbm.21387

Eden, D. (2001). Means efficacy: External
sources of general and specific subjective
efficacy. In M. Erez, U. Kleinbeck, & H. Thierry
(Eds.), *Work Motivation in the Context of a
Globalizing Economy* (p73–85). Lawrence
Erlbaum Associates Publishers

Luszczynska, A., Gutiérrez-Doña, B., &
Schwarzer, R. (2005). General self-efficacy
in various domains of human functioning:
Evidence from five countries. *International
Journal of Psychology*, 40(2), 80-89

109. Lilien, G. L., Morrison, P. D., Searls, K., Sonnack,
M., & Hippel, E. V. (2002). Performance
assessment of the lead user idea-generation
process for new product development.
Management Science, 48(8), 1042-1059

110. Kolb, D. A. (1984). Learning cycle and learning style inventory. DA Kolb, *Experiential Learning*. London: Prentice Hall

111. Tsang, Organizational learning and the learning organization: a dichotomy between descriptive and prescriptive research

112. Kontoghiorghes et al., Learning organization characteristics

113. Goh et al., Learning capability and organizational performance

114. Kontoghiorghes et al., Learning organization characteristics

115. Rose et al., The effect of organizational learning

116. Carmeli & Gittell, High-quality relationships; Edmondson, Psychological Safety and Learning Behavior in Work Teams, p350; Edmondson, Psychological safety, trust, and learning in organizations

117. Li & Yan, The effects of trust climate on individual performance

118. Hersey, P., Blanchard, K., & Johnson D. (1996). Management of organizational behavior: Utilizing human resources, 7th edition. Prentice Hall, Upper Saddle River, N.J

119. Dweck & Leggett, A social-cognitive approach to motivation and personality

120. Dweck & Leggett, A social-cognitive approach to motivation and personality; Aditomo, Students' Response to Academic Setback; Ng, The neuroscience of growth mindset and intrinsic motivation, p20

121. Schuitema, *Leadership: The Care and Growth Model*

122. Argyris, Good communication that blocks learning; Kolb, *The Kolb learning style inventory*

123. Haapakangas et al., Benefits of quiet workspaces in open-plan offices

124. www.dictionary.com, accessed February 2021

125. Edmondson, Psychological Safety and Learning Behavior in Work Teams, p350; Kahn, Personal Engagement and Disengagement at Work; Detert & Burris, Leadership behavior and employee voice; Walumbwa & Schaubroeck, Leader Personality Traits and Employee Voice Behavior; Schaubroeck et al., Leader Behavior Influences on Team Performance; Coombe, *Secure base leadership*; Madjar & Ortiz-Walters, Trust in Supervisors and Trust in Customers; Frazier et al., Psychological Safety; Maslach et al., Job burnout

126. Kahn, Personal Engagement and Disengagement at Work, p708

127. Chamorro-Premuzic, *Why Do So Many Incompetent Men Become Leaders?*

128. Edmondson, A. (1999). Psychological Safety and Learning Behavior in Work Teams. *Administrative Science Quarterly, 44*(2), 350–383. doi: 10.2307/2666999

Kahn, W. A. (1990). Psychological Conditions of Personal Engagement and Disengagement at Work. *Academy of Management Journal, 33*(4), 692–724. doi: 10.2307/256287

Mather, S. (2020). The Contribution of Psychological Resources in the Creation of Employee Safety. (PhD), University of Reading, England

129. Taylor & Small, Asking applicants what they would do versus what they did do

130. www.clickboarding.com, May 2020

131. Toor & Rehman, Authenticity and its influence on psychological well-being; Ryan et al., Self-Complexity and the Authenticity of Self-Aspects

132. Metin et al., Authenticity at work

133. Creswell et al., Affirmation of Personal Values

134. Higgins, Self-Discrepancy, 21

References

Aditomo, A. (2015). Students' Response to Academic Setback: 'Growth Mindset' as a Buffer against Demotivation. *International Journal of Educational Psychology*, 4(2), 198–222

Albarracín, D., & Kumkale, G. T. (2003). Affect as information in persuasion: A model of affect identification and discounting. *Journal of Personality and Social Psychology*, 84(3), 453–469. doi: 10.1037/0022-3514.84.3.453

Alegre, I., Berbegal-Mirabent, J., Guerrero, A., & Mas-Machuca, M. (2018). The real mission of the mission statement: A systematic review of the literature. *Journal of Management & Organization*, 24(4), 456–473

Argyris. (1994). Good communication that blocks learning. *Harvard Business Review*, 77–85(4)

Arnsten, A. F. T., Raskind, M. A., Taylor, F. B., & Connor, D. F. (2015). The effects of stress exposure on prefrontal cortex: Translating basic research into successful treatments for post-traumatic stress disorder. *Neurobiology of Stress*, 89–99, 10. http://dx.doi.org/10.1016/j.ynstr.2014.10.002

Asongu, S. A. (2015). Financial Sector Competition and Knowledge Economy: Evidence from SSA and MENA Countries. *Journal of the Knowledge Economy*, 6(4), 717–748. doi: 10.1007/s13132-012-0141-4

Aspinwall, L. G., Richter, L., & Hoffman, R. (2001). Understanding how optimism works: An examination of optimists' adaptive moderation of belief and behavior. In E. C. Chang (Ed.), *Optimism and pessimism: Implications for theory, research, and practice*, 217–238. Washington, D.C.: American Psychological Association

Atouba, Y. C., & Lammers, J. C. (2018). Examining the relationships between participative organisational communication practices and burnout among IT professionals. *Total Quality Management & Business Excellence*, 31(7–8), 1–15

Auvinen, T., Aaltio, I., & Blomqvist, K. (2013). Constructing leadership by storytelling – the meaning of trust and narratives. *Leadership & Organization*

Development Journal, 34(6), 496–514. doi: 10.1108/ LODJ-10-2011-0102

Baard, S. K., Rench, T. A., & Kozlowski, S. W. J. (2014). Performance Adaptation. *Journal of Management*, 40(1), 48–99. doi: 10.1177/0149206313488210

Baldoni, J. (2011), Purpose Is What Your Organization Needs Most. Here's How to Get It. *Forbes Leadership Forum*. www.forbes.com/sites/forbes leadershipforum/2011/11/07/purpose-is-what-your-organization-needs-most-heres-how-to-get-it, accessed February 2021

Bandura, A. (1986). Fearful expectations and avoidant actions as coeffects of perceived self-inefficacy. *American Psychologist* (December), 1389–1391

Bandura, A. (1997). *Self-efficacy: The exercise of control.* Macmillan

Bandura, A., & Locke, E. A. (2003). Negative self-efficacy and goal effects revisited. *Journal of Applied Psychology*, 88(1), 87–99. doi: 10.1037/ 0021-9010.88.1.87

Bandura, A., & Wood, R. (1989). Effect of Perceived Controllability and Performance Standards on Self-Regulation of Complex Decision-Making. *Journal of Personality and Social Psychology*, 56(5), 805–814. doi: 10.1037//0022-3514.56.5.805

Baumeister, R. F., Dori, G. A., & Hastings, S. (1998). Belongingness and temporal bracketing in personal accounts of changes in self-esteem. *Journal of Research in Personality*, 32(2), 222–235. doi: 10.1006/ jrpe.1998.2218

Baumeister, R. F., Muraven, M., & Tice, D. M. (2000). Ego depletion: A resource model of volition, self-regulation, and controlled processing. *Social Cognition*, 18(2), 130–150. doi: 10.1521/ soco.2000.18.2.130

Baumeister, R. F., & Vohs, K. D. (2002). The pursuit of meaningfulness in life. *Handbook of Positive Psychology*, 1, 608–618

Baumeister, R. F., Vohs, K. D., & Tice, D. M. (2007). The strength model of self-control. *Current Directions in Psychological Science*, 16(6), 351–355

Beechler, S., & Woodward, I. C. (2009). The global 'war for talent'. *Journal of International Management*, 15(3), 273–285. doi: 10.1016/j.intman.2009.01.002

Beltman, S., Mansfield, C., & Price, A. (2011). Thriving not just surviving: A review of research on teacher resilience. *Educational Research Review*, 6(3), 186. doi: 10.1016/j.edurev.2011.09.001

Bennett, N., & Lemoine, G. J. (2014). What a difference a word makes: Understanding threats to performance in a VUCA world. *Business Horizons*, 57(3), 311–317. doi: 10.1016/j.bushor.2014.01.001

Bennett, N., & Lemoine, J. (2014). What VUCA really means for you. *Harvard Business Review*, 92(1/2). 27

Bensimon, M. (2012). Elaboration on the association between trauma, PTSD and posttraumatic growth: The role of trait resilience. *Personality and Individual Differences*, 52(7), 782–787. doi: 10.1016/j.paid. 2012.01.011

Bodenhausen, G. V., Kramer, G. P., & Susser, K. (1994). Happiness and stereotypic thinking in social judgment. *Journal of Personality and Social Psychology*, 66(4), 621–632. doi: 10.1037/0022-3514.66.4.621

Bohner, G., Erb, H.-P., & Siebler, F. (2008). Information Processing Approaches to Persuasion: Integrating Assumptions from the Dual- and Single-Processing Perspectives. In W. D. Crano & R. Prislin (Eds.), *Attitudes and attitude change*, 161–189. New York: Taylor and Francis

Bonanno, G. A. (2004). Loss, trauma, and human resilience – Have we underestimated the human capacity to thrive after extremely aversive events? *American Psychologist*, 59(1), 20–28. doi: 10.1037/ 0003-066x.59.1.20

Bonanno, G. A. (2005). Resilience in the face of potential trauma. *Current Directions in Psychological Science*, 14(3), 135–138

Bonanno, G. A., Boerner, K., & Wortman, C. B. (2008). Trajectories of grieving. In *Handbook of Bereavement Research and Practice: Advances in Theory and Intervention*, 287–307. Cambridge University Press, Cambridge, UK

Bowen, S. A. (2018). Mission and Vision. *The International Encyclopedia of Strategic Communication*, 1–9. Wiley Press

Britt, T. W., Shen, W., Sinclair, R. R., Grossman, M. R., & Klieger, D. M. (2016). How Much Do We Really Know About Employee Resilience? *Industrial and Organizational Psychology*, 9(02), 378–404. doi: 10.1017/iop.2015.107

Buhler, P. M. (2011). Changing organizational structures and their impact on managers. *Supervision*, 72(2), 24–26

Cacioppo, J. T., Cacioppo, S., & Petty, R. E. (2018). The neuroscience of persuasion: A review with an emphasis on issues and opportunities. *Social Neuroscience*, 13(2), 129–172. doi: 10.1080/17470919.2016.1273851

Cacioppo, J. T., Gardner, W. L., & Berntson, G. G. (1999). The affect system has parallel and integrative processing components: Form follows function. *Journal of Personality and Social Psychology, 76*(5), 839–855. doi: 10.1037/0022-3514.76.5.839

Carmeli, A., & Gittell, J. H. (2009). High-quality relationships, psychological safety, and learning from failures in work organizations. *Journal of Organizational Behavior, 30*(6), 709–729. doi: 10.1002/job.565

Cartwright, S. (2003). New forms of work organization: Issues and challenges. *Leadership & Organization Development Journal, 24*(3), 121–122. doi: 10.1108/01437730310469534

Carver, C. S., Pozo, C., Harris, S. D., Noriega, V., Scheier, M. F., Robinson, D. S., Ketcham, A. S., Moffat, F. L., and Clark, K. C. (1993). How Coping Mediates the Effect of Optimism on Distress – a Study of Women with Early-Stage Breast-Cancer. *Journal of Personality and Social Psychology, 65*(2), 375–390. doi: 10.1037/0022-3514.65.2.375

Carver, C. S., & Scheier, M. F. (1990). Origins and Functions of Positive and Negative Affect – a Control-Process View. *Psychological Review, 97*(1), 19–35. doi: 10.1037/0033-295x.97.1.19

Caza, B. B., & Milton, L. P. (2012). Resilience at work. In *The Oxford Handbook of Positive Organizational Scholarship.* Oxford University Press, New York.

Cervone, D. (1991). Goal setting and the differential influence of self-regulatory processes on complex decision-making performance. *Journal of Personality and Social Psychology*, 61(2), 257–266. doi: 10.1037/0022-3514.61.2.257

Chamorro-Premuzic, T. (2019). *Why Do So Many Incompetent Men Become Leaders?* Harvard Business Review Press, Boston, MA

Chan, D. (2000). Understanding Adaptation to Changes in the Work Environment: Integrating Individual Difference and Learning Perspectives. In G. R. Ferris (Ed.) *Research in Personnel and Human Resources Management*, 18, 1–42. Greenwich, CT: JAI Press

Ciulla, J. B. (2005). The state of leadership ethics and the work that lies before us. *Business Ethics: A European Review*, 12, 323–335

Clore, G. L., & Huntsinger, J. R. (2007). How emotions inform judgment and regulate thought. *Trends in Cognitive Sciences*, 11(9), 393–399. doi: 10.1016/j.tics.2007.08.005

Compas, B. E. (2006). Psychobiological processes of stress and coping – Implications for resilience in children and adolescents – Comments on the papers of Romeo & McEwen and Fisher et al. New York Academy of Sciences 1094(1), 226–234. doi: 10.1196/annals.1376.024

Coombe, D. D. (2010). *Secure base leadership: A positive theory of leadership incorporating safety, exploration and positive action.* Case Western Reserve University, Cleveland, Ohio

Cousins, B. (2018). Design thinking: Organizational Learning in VUCA Environments. *Academy of Strategic Management Journal*, 1–18(2)

Cozzarelli, C. (1993). Personality and self-efficacy as predictors of coping with abortion. *Journal of Personality and Social Psychology*, 65(6), 1224–1236. doi: 10.1037/0022-3514.65.6.1224

Creswell, J. D., Welch, W. T., Taylor, S. E., Sherman, D. K., Gruenewald, T. L., & Mann, T. (2005). Affirmation of Personal Values Buffers Neuroendocrine and Psychological Stress Responses. *Psychological Science*, 16(11), 846–851. doi: 10.1111/j.1467- 9280.2005.01624.x

De Meuse, K. P. (2010). Learning agility: A construct whose time has come. *Consulting Psychology Journal*, 62(2), 119–130. doi: 10.1037/a0019988

De Smet, A., Lund, S., & Schaninger, W. (2016). Organizing for the future. *McKinsey Quarterly*, January 2016, 2–14

De Witte, H., Pienaar, J., & De Cuyper, N. (2016). Review of 30 years of longitudinal studies on the association between job insecurity and health and well-being: Is there causal evidence? *Australian Psychologist*, 51(1), 18–31

Denning, S. (2006). Effective storytelling: Strategic business narrative techniques. *Strategy & Leadership*, 34(1), 42–48. doi: 10.1108/10878570610637885

Detert, J. R., & Burris, E. R. (2007). Leadership behavior and employee voice: Is the door really open? *Academy of Management Journal*, 50(4), 869–884

Direnzo, M. S., & Greenhaus, J. H. (2011). Job Search and Voluntary Turnover in a Boundaryless World: A Control Theory Perspective. *Academy of Management Review*, 36(3), 567–589. doi: 10.5465/Amr.2011.61031812

Dweck, C. S., & Leggett, E. L. (1988). A social-cognitive approach to motivation and personality. *Psychological Review*, 95(2), 256–273. doi: 10.1037/0033-295X.95.2.256

Eden, D., & Ravid, G. (1982). Pygmalion Versus Self-Expectancy – Effects of Instructor-Expectancy and Self-Expectancy on Trainee Performance. *Organizational Behavior and Human Performance*, 30(3), 351–364. doi: 10.1016/0030-5073(82)90225-2

Edmondson, A. (1999). Psychological Safety and Learning Behavior in Work Teams. *Administrative Science Quarterly*, 44(2), 350–383. doi: 10.2307/2666999

Edmondson, A. C. (2003). Psychological safety, trust, and learning in organizations: A group-level lens. *Trust and Distrust in Organizations: Dilemmas and Approaches*, 12, 239–272

Edmondson, A. C., & Harvey, J.-F. (2017). Cross-boundary teaming for innovation: Integrating research on teams and knowledge in organizations. *Human Resource Management Review*, 28(4), 347–360. doi: 10.1016/j.hrmr.2017.03.002

Egeland, B., Carlson, E., & Sroufe, L. A. (1993). Resilience as Process. *Development and Psychopathology*, 5(4), 517–528

Faraj, S., & Yan, A. (2009). Boundary work in knowledge teams. *Journal of Applied Psychology*, 94(3), 604–617. doi: 10.1037/a0014367

Francis, Z., & Job, V. (2018). Lay theories of willpower. *Social and Personality Psychology Compass*, 12(4), e12381

Frazier, M. L., Fainshmidt, S., Klinger, R. L., Pezeshkan, A., & Vracheva, V. (2017). Psychological Safety: A Meta-Analytic Review and Extension. *Personnel Psychology*, 70(1), 113–165. doi: 10.1111/peps.12183

Frazier, P., Tennen, H., Gavian, M., Park, C., Tomich, P., & Tashiro, T. (2009). Does Self-Reported Post-traumatic Growth Reflect Genuine Positive Change? *Psychological Science*, 20(7), 912–919

Garland, H. (1983). Influence of ability, assigned goals, and normative information on personal goals and performance: A challenge to the goal attainability assumption. *Journal of Applied Psychology*, 68(1), 20–30. doi: 10.1037/0021-9010.68.1.20

Garland, H. (1985). A Cognitive Mediation Theory of Task Goals and Human Performance. *Motivation and Emotion*, 9(4), 345–367. doi: 10.1007/Bf00992205

Garmezy, N. (1991). Resilience in Children's Adaptation to Negative Life Events and Stressed Environments. *Pediatric Annals*, 20(9), 459–466

Gawronski, B., & Bodenhausen, G. V. (2006). Associative and propositional processes in evaluation: An integrative review of implicit and explicit attitude change. *Psychological Bulletin*, 132(5), 692–731. doi: 10.1037/0033-2909.132.5.692

Gibson, C. B., & Gibbs, J. L. (2006). Unpacking the Concept of Virtuality: The Effects of Geographic Dispersion, Electronic Dependence, Dynamic Structure, and National Diversity on Team Innovation. *Administrative Science Quarterly*, 51(3), 451–495. doi: 10.2189/asqu.51.3.451

Girotti, M., Adler, S. M., Bulin, S. E., Fucich, E. A., Paredes, D., & Morilak, D. A. (2018). Prefrontal cortex executive processes affected by stress in health and disease. *Progress in Neuro-Psychopharmacology & Biological Psychiatry*, 85, 161–179. doi: 10.1016/j.pnpbp.2017.07.004

Glantz, M. D., & Sloboda, Z. (2002). Analysis and Reconceptualization of Resilience. In M. D. Glantz & J. L. Johnson (Eds.), *Resilience and Development: Positive Life Adaptations*, 109–126. Boston, MA: Springer US

Goh, S. C., Elliott, C., & Quon, T. K. (2012). The relationship between learning capability and organizational performance: A meta-analytic examination. *The Learning Organization*, 19(2), 92–108. doi: 10.1108/09696471211201461

Gordon, K. A. (1995). Self-Concept and Motivational Patterns of Resilient African American High School Students. *Journal of Black Psychology*, 21(3), 239–255. doi: 10.1177/00957984950213003

Gordon, K. A., & Coscarelli, W. C. (1996). Recognizing and fostering resilience. *Performance Improvement*, 35(9), 14–17

Guest, D. E. (2017). Human resource management and employee well-being: Towards a new analytic framework. *Human Resource Management Journal*, 27(1), 22–38

Gulotta, B., Sadia, G., & Sussman, E. (2013). Emotional processing modulates attentional capture of irrelevant sound input in adolescents. *International Journal of Psychophysiology*, 88(1), 40–46

Haapakangas, A., Hongisto, V., Varjo, J., & Lahtinen, M. (2018). Benefits of quiet workspaces in open-plan offices – Evidence from two office relocations. *Journal of Environmental Psychology*, 56, 63–75. doi: 10.1016/j. jenvp.2018.03.003

Hackman, J. R., & Oldham, G. R. (1976). Motivation through the Design of Work: Test of a Theory. *Organizational Behavior and Human Performance*, 16(2), 250–279. doi: 10.1016/0030-5073(76)90016-7

Harris, J., & Barnes, B. K. (2006). Leadership storytelling. *Industrial and Commercial Training*, 38(7), 350–353. doi: 10.1108/00197850610704534

Haskel, J., & Martin, C. (2001). Technology, wages, and skill shortages: evidence from UK micro data. *Oxford Economic Papers – New Series*, 53(4), 642–658. doi: 10.1093/oep/53.4.642

Heerwagen, J., Kelly, K., & Kampschroer, K. (2016). The Changing Nature of Organizations, Work, and Workplace. www.wbdg.org/resources/changing-nature-organizations-work-and-workplace, accessed 12 February 2021

Helgeson, V. S., Reynolds, K. A., & Tomich, P. L. (2006). A meta-analytic review of benefit finding and growth. *Journal of Consulting and Clinical Psychology*, 74(5), 797–816. doi: 10.1037/0022-006X.74.5.797

Higgins, E. T. (1987). Self-Discrepancy: A Theory Relating Self and Affect. *Psychological Review*, 94(3), 319–340

Hobfoll, S. E. (1989). Conservation of Resources – a New Attempt at Conceptualizing Stress. *American Psychologist*, 44(3), 513–524. doi: 10.1037/0003-066x.44.3.513

Hobfoll, S. E. (2002). Social and psychological resources and adaptation. *Review of General Psychology*, 6(4), 307–324. doi: 10.1037//1089-2680.6.4.307

Hohnen, B., & Murphy, T. (2016). The optimum context for learning: Drawing on neuroscience to inform best practice in the classroom. *Educational and Child Psychology*, 75–90(1)

Holahan, C. J., Moos, R. H., Holahan, C. K., & Cronkite, R. C. (1999). Resource loss, resource gain, and depressive symptoms: A 10-year model. *Journal of Personality and Social Psychology*, 77(3), 620–629. doi: 10.1037/0022-3514.77.3.620

Hovland, C. I., & Harvey, O. J., & Sherif, M. M. (1957). Assimilation and contrast effects in reactions to communication and attitude change. *Journal of Abnormal and Social Psychology*, 55(2), 244–252. doi: 10.1037/h0048480

Huntsinger, J. R., Isbell, L. M., & Clore, G. L. (2014). The affective control of thought: Malleable, not fixed. *Psychological Review*, 121(4), 600–618. doi: 10.1037/a0037669

Hurth, V., Ebert, C., & Prabhu, J. (2018). Organisational purpose: the construct and its antecedents and consequences. *Cambridge Judge Business School Working Papers*, 2–67

Isbell, L. M., Burns, K. C., & Haar, T. (2005). The role of affect on the search for global and specific target information. *Social Cognition*, 23(6), 529–552

Isen, A. M., Daubman, K. A., & Nowicki, G. P. (1987). Positive affect facilitates creative problem solving. *Journal of Personality and Social Psychology*, 52(6), 1122–1131. doi: 10.1037/0022-3514.52.6.1122

Jensen, S., Luthans, K. W., Lebsack, S. A., & Lebsack, R. R. (2007). Optimism and employee performance in the banking industry. *The Journal of Applied Management and Entrepreneurship*, 12(3), 57–72

Job, V., Dweck, C. S., & Walton, G. M. (2010).
Ego depletion – is it all in your head? Implicit
theories about willpower affect self-regulation.
Psychological Science, 21(11), 1686–1693. doi:
10.1177/0956797610384745

Johnson, S. (1999). *Who Moved My Cheese? An
A-Mazing Way to Deal with Change in Your Work and
in Your Life*. Vermillion, London

Joseph, S., Williams, R., & Yule, W. (1993). Changes in
outlook following disaster: The preliminary development of a measure to assess positive and negative
responses. *Journal of Traumatic Stress*, 6(2), 271–279.
doi: 10.1002/jts.2490060209

Kahn, W. A. (1990). Psychological Conditions of
Personal Engagement and Disengagement at Work.
Academy of Management Journal, 33(4), 692–724.
doi: 10.2307/256287

Kalisch, R., Cramer, A. O., Binder, H., Fritz, J., Leer-
touwer, I., Lunansky, G., Meyer, B., Timmer, J., Feer,
I. M. and Van Harmelen, A.-L. (2019). Deconstructing
and reconstructing resilience: a dynamic network
approach. *Perspectives on Psychological Science*, 14(5),
765–777

Kaplan, R. S., & Norton, D. P. (1992). *The Balanced
Scorecard: Translating Strategy Into Action*. Harvard
Business Review Press, USA

Keinan, G., Friedland, N., Kahneman, D., & Roth, D. (1999). The effect of stress on the suppression of erroneous competing responses. *Anxiety, Stress & Coping*, 12(4), 455–476

King, D. W., King, L. A., Foy, D. W., Keane, T. M., & Fairbank, J. A. (1999). Posttraumatic stress disorder in a national sample of female and male Vietnam veterans. Risk factors, war-zone stressors, and resilience-recovery variables. *Journal of Abnormal Psychology*, 108(1), 164–170. doi: 10.1037/0021-843x.108.1.164

Klein, C. T. F., & Helweg-Larsen, M. (2002). Perceived Control and the Optimistic Bias: A Meta-Analytic Review. *Psychology & Health*, 17(4), 437–446. doi: 10.1080/0887044022000004920

Kolb, D. A. (2007). *The Kolb learning style inventory*. Boston, MA: Hay Resources Direct

Kontoghiorghes, C., Awbre, S. M., & Feurig, P. L. (2005). Examining the relationship between learning organization characteristics and change adaptation, innovation, and organizational performance. *Human Resource Development Quarterly*, 16(2), 185–212

Kumpfer, K. L. (2002). Factors and processes contributing to resilience. In *Resilience and Development*, 179–224. Springer. New York

Lang, P. J. (1995). The Emotion Probe – Studies of Motivation and Attention. *American Psychologist*, 50(5), 372–385. doi: 10.1037//0003-066x.50.5.372

Lazarus, R. S., & Folkman, S. (1987). Transactional theory and research on emotions and coping. *European Journal of Personality*, 1(3), 141–169. doi: 10.1002/per.2410010304

Li, A., & Bagger, J. (2008). Role ambiguity and self-efficacy: The moderating effects of goal orientation and procedural justice. *Journal of Vocational Behavior*, 73(3), 368–375. doi: 10.1016/j.jvb.2008.07.008

Li, N., & Yan, J. (2009). The effects of trust climate on individual performance. *Frontiers of Business Research in China*, 3(1), 27–49. doi: 10.1007/s11782-009-0002-6

Lilien, G. L., Morrison, P. D., Searls, K., Sonnack, M., & Hippel, E. V. (2002). Performance assessment of the lead user idea-generation process for new product development. *Management Science*, 48(8), 1042–1059

Locke, E. A., & Latham, G. P. (1990). Work motivation and satisfaction: Light at the end of the tunnel. *Psychological Science*, 1(4), 240–246

Locke, E. A., & Latham, G. P. (2006). New directions in goal-setting theory. *Current Directions in Psychological Science*, 15(5), 265–268

Luthans, F. (2002). Positive organizational behavior: Developing and managing psychological strengths. *Academy of Management Executive*, 16(1), 57–72

Luthar, S. S., Cicchetti, D., & Becker, B. (2000). The Construct of Resilience: A Critical Evaluation and Guidelines for Future Work. *Child Development*, 71(3), 543–562. doi: 10.1111/1467-8624.00164

Madjar, N., & Ortiz-Walters, R. (2009). Trust in Supervisors and Trust in Customers: Their Independent, Relative, and Joint Effects on Employee Performance and Creativity. *Human Performance*, 22(2), 128–142. doi: 10.1080/08959280902743501

Marois, R. & Ivanoff, J. (2005). Capacity Limits of Information Processing in the Brain. *Trends in Cognitive Sciences*, 9(6), 296–305

Maslach, C. (2003). *Burnout: The Cost of Caring*. Cambridge, MA: Malor Books.

Maslach, C., Schaufeli, W. B., & Leiter, M. P. (2001). Job burnout. *Annual Review of Psychology*, 52, 397–422. doi: 10.1146/annurev.psych.52.1.397

Masten, A. S. (2001). Ordinary magic – Resilience processes in development. *American Psychologist*, 56(3), 227–238. doi: 10.1037//0003-066x.56.3.227

Masten, A. S., Best, K. M., & Garmezy, N. (1990). Resilience and development: Contributions from the study of children who overcome adversity. *Development and Psychopathology*, 2(4), 425–444

Mather, S. (2020). The Contribution of Psychological Resources in the Creation of Employee Safety. (PhD), University of Reading, England

Masterson, F, A., & Crawford, M. (1984). The defence motivation system: A theory of avoidance behaviour. *Behavioural and Brain Sciences 5* (04):661–675. doi: 10.1017/S0140525X00014114

McArthur, A. (June 2016). Beating VUCA's Whiplash Factor. *Talent Development Magazine*, 70–73

McEwen, B. S. (2001). Plasticity of the Hippocampus: Adaptation to Chronic Stress and Allostatic Load. *Annals of the New York Academy of Sciences*, 933(1), 265–277. doi: 10.1111/j.1749-6632.2001.tb05830.x

McEwen, B. S. (2016). In pursuit of resilience: stress, epigenetics, and brain plasticity. *Annals of the New York Academy of Sciences*, 1373(1), 56–64. doi: 10.1111/nyas.13020

McEwen, B. S., & Gianaros, P. J. (2010). Central role of the brain in stress and adaptation: Links to socioeconomic status, health, and disease. *Biology of*

Disadvantage: Socioeconomic Status and Health, 1186, 190–222. doi: 10.1111/j.1749- 6632.2009.05331.x

McEwen, B., & Sapolsky, R. M. (1995). Stress and Cognitive Function. *Current Opinion in Neurobiology*, 5(2), 205–216

McKenna, F. P. (1993). It won't happen to me: Unrealistic optimism or illusion of control? *The British Journal of Psychology*, 84(1), 39–50. doi: 10.1111/j.2044-8295.1993.tb02461.x

McNeil, K. A., Mitchell, R. J., & Parker, V. (2013). Interprofessional practice and professional identity threat. *Health Sociology Review*, 22(3), 291–307

Meredith, L. S., Sherbourne, C. D., Gaillot, S. J., Hansell, L., Ritschard, H. V., Parker, A. M., & Wrenn, G. (2011). Promoting Psychological Resilience in the U.S. Military. *Rand Health Quarterly*, 1(2), 2

Metin, U. B., Taris, T. W., Peeters, M. C. W., van Beek, I., & van den Bosch, R. (2016). Authenticity at work – a job-demands resources perspective. *Journal of Managerial Psychology*, 31(2), 483–499. doi: 10.1108/Jmp-03-2014-0087

Mohrman, S. A. (1999). The contexts for geographically dispersed teams and networks. *Journal of Organizational Behavior*, 6, 63–80

Muraven, M., & Baumeister, F. (2000). Self-regulation and depletion of limited resources: Does self-control resemble a muscle? *Psychological Bulletin*, 126(2), 247–259. doi: 10.1037/0033-2909.126.2.247

Muraven., M., Shmueli, D., & Burkley, E. (2006). Conserving Self-Control Strength. *Journal of Personality and Social Psychology*, 91(3 September 2006), 13, 524–537

Näswall, K., Kuntz, J., Hodliffe, M., & Malinen, S. (2015). *Employee Resilience Scale (EmpRes) Measurement Properties.* Resilient Organisations Research Report 2015/04, www.resorgs.org.nz, accessed February 2021

Ng, B. (2018). The neuroscience of growth mindset and intrinsic motivation. *Brain Sciences*, 8(2), 20–30

Norris, F. H., & Kaniasty, K. (1996). Received and perceived social support in times of stress: A test of the social support deterioration deterrence model. *Journal of Personality and Social Psychology*, 71(3), 498–511. doi: 10.1037/0022-3514.71.3.498

Pargament, K. I., & Park, C. L. (1995). Merely a Defense? The Variety of Religious Means and Ends. *Journal of Social Issues*, 51(2), 13–32. doi: 10.1111/j.1540-4560.1995.tb01321.x

Park, C. L. (1998). Implications of posttraumatic growth for individuals. In *Posttraumatic Growth: Positive Changes in the Aftermath of Crisis*, 153–177. Taylor and Francis, New Jersey

Peters, T. (1990) Get Innovative or Get Dead. *Californian Management Review*, 33(2), 9–23

Peterson, C. (2000). The future of optimism. *American Psychologist*, 55(1), 44–55. doi: 10.1037//0003-066x.55.1.44

Petty, R. E., & Briñol, P. (2015). Emotion and persuasion: Cognitive and meta-cognitive processes impact attitudes. *Cognition and Emotion*, 29(1), 1–26. doi: 10.1080/02699931.2014.967183

Ployhart, R. E., & Bliese, P. D. (2006). Individual adaptability (I-ADAPT) theory: Conceptualizing the antecedents, consequences, and measurement of individual differences in adaptability. In *Understanding adaptability: A prerequisite for effective performance within complex environments*, 3–39. Emerald Group Publishing Limited

Pulakos, E. D. (2015). Performance Management Can Be Fixed: An On-the-Job Experiential Learning Approach for Complex Behavior Change. *Industrial and Organizational Psychology*, 8(01), 51–76. doi: 10.1017/iop.2014.2

Quinn, R. E., & Thankor, A. V. (2018). Creating a Purpose-Driven Organization. *Harvard Business Review* (July-August), 78–85

Ready, D. A. (2002). How storytelling builds next-generation leaders. *MIT Sloan Management Review*, 43(4), 63–69

Rich, H. (December 2018). On the streets: an investigation into rough sleeping (Summary Report). Shelter – The housing and homelessness charity. https://england.shelter.org.uk/professional_resources/policy_and_research/policy_library/policy_library_folder/research_on_the_streets_-_an_investigation_into_rough_sleeping, accessed 12 February 2021

Richardson, G. E. (2002). The metatheory of resilience and resiliency. *Journal of Clinical Psychology*, 58(3), 307–321. doi: 10.1002/jclp.10020

Rini, C. K., Dunkel-Schetter, C., Wadhwa, P. D., & Sandman, C. A. (1999). Psychological adaptation and birth outcomes: The role of personal resources, stress, and sociocultural context in pregnancy. *Health Psychology*, 18(4), 333–345. doi: 10.1037/0278- 6133.18.4.333

Rogers, T. J., Alderman, B. L., & Landers, D. M. (2003). Effects of life-event stress and hardiness on peripheral vision in a real-life stress situation. *Behavioural Medicine*, 29(1), 21–26

Rose, R. C., Kumar, N., & Pak, O. G. (2009). The effect of organizational learning on organizational commitment, job satisfaction and work performance. *Journal of Applied Business Research (JABR)*, 25(6), 55–66

Rutter, M. (1987). Psychosocial resilience and protective mechanisms. *American Journal of Orthopsychiatry*, 57(3), 316–331. doi: 10.1111/j.1939-0025.1987. tb03541.x

Ryan, R. M., LaGuardia, J. G., & Rawsthorne, L. J. (2005). Self-Complexity and the Authenticity of Self-Aspects: Effects on Well Being and Resilience to Stressful Events. *North American Journal of Psychology*, 7(3), 431–447

Ryff, C. D., & Singer, B. (2003). Flourishing under fire: Resilience as a prototype of challenged thriving. In *Flourishing: Positive Psychology and the Life Well-Lived*, 15–36. American Psychological Association, United States

Schabracq, M. J., & Cooper, C. L. (2000). The changing nature of work and stress. *Journal of Managerial Psychology*, 15(3), 227–241. doi: 10.1108/02683940010320589

Schaubroeck, J., Lam, S. S. K., & Peng, A. C. Y. (2011). Cognition-Based and Affect-Based Trust as Mediators of Leader Behavior Influences on Team Performance. *Journal of Applied Psychology*, 96(4), 863–871. doi: 10.1037/a0022625

Scheier, M. F., & Carver, C. S. (1985). Optimism, Coping, and Health – Assessment and Implications of Generalized Outcome Expectancies. *Health Psychology*, 4(3), 219–247. doi: 10.1037//0278-6133.4.3.219

Scheier, M. F., Weintraub, J. K., & Carver, C. S. (1986). Coping with stress: Divergent strategies of optimists and pessimists. *Journal of Personality and Social Psychology*, 51(6), 1257–1264. doi: 10.1037/0022-3514.51.6.1257

Schuitema, E. (2000). *Leadership: The Care and Growth Model*. Kenilworth, South Africa: Ampersand Press

Schuler, R. S., Jackson, S. E., & Tarique, I. (2011). Global talent management and global talent challenges: Strategic opportunities for IHRM. *Journal of World Business*, 46, 506–515

Schwarz, N., & Clore, G. L. (1983). Mood, misattribution, and judgments of well-being: Informative and directive functions of affective states. *Journal of Personality and Social Psychology*, 45(3), 513–523. doi: 10.1037/0022-3514.45.3.513

Segerstrom, S. C., Taylor, S. E., Kemeny, M. E., & Fahey, J. L. (1998). Optimism is associated with mood, coping, and immune change in response to stress. *Journal of Personality and Social Psychology*, 74(6), 1646–1655. doi: 10.1037/0022-3514.74.6.1646

Seligman, M. E. (2006). *Learned Optimism: How to Change Your Mind and Your Life.* Simon and Schuster, New York

Seligman, M. E., & Csikszentmihalyi, M. (2000). Positive psychology: An introduction. *American Psychologist,* 55(1), 5–14

Sharkie, R. (2005). Precariousness under the new psychological contract: the effect on trust and the willingness to converse and share knowledge. *Knowledge Management Research & Practice,* 3(1), 37–44. doi: 10.1057/palgrave.kmrp.8500051

Simpson, J. A. (2007). Psychological foundations of trust. *Current Directions in Psychological Science,* 16(5), 264–268. doi: 10.1111/j.1467-8721.2007.00517.x

Small, D., Loewenstein, G., & Slovic, P. (2007) Sympathy and callousness: The impact of deliberative thought on donations to identifiable and statistical victims. *Organizational Behavior and Human Decision Processes,* 102(2), 143–153

Snyder, C. R., Sympson, S. C., Michael, S. T., & Cheavens, J. (2001). Optimism and hope constructs: Variants on a positive expectancy theme. In *Optimism and Pessimism: Implications for Theory, Research, and Practice,* 101–125. American Psychological Association, United States

Sommer, S. A. (2016). Keeping Positive and Building Strength: The Role of Affect and Team Leadership in Developing Resilience During an Organizational Crisis. *Group & Organization Management*, 41(2), 172–202. doi: 10.1177/1059601115578027

Stajkovic, A. D., & Luthans, F. (1998). Social cognitive theory and self-efficacy: Going beyond traditional motivational and behavioral approaches. *Organizational Dynamics*, 26(4), 62–74. doi: 10.1016/S0090-2616(98)90006-7

Staudinger, U. M., Marsiske, M., & Baltes, P. B. (1993). Resilience and Levels of Reserve Capacity in Later Adulthood – Perspectives from Life-Span Theory. *Development and Psychopathology*, 5(4), 541–566

Sutcliffe, K. M., & Vogus, T. J. (2003). Organizing for resilience. In *Positive Organizational Scholarship*, 94–110

Sweldens, S., Corneille, O., & Yzerbyt, V. (2014). The Role of Awareness in Attitude Formation Through Evaluative Conditioning. *Personality and Social Psychology Review*, 18(2), 187–209. doi: 10.1177/1088868314527832

Taylor, P. J., & Small, B. (2000). Asking applicants what they would do versus what they did do: A meta-analytical comparison of situations and past behaviour employment interview questions. *Journal of Occupational and Organizational Psychology*, 75(3), 277–294

Tedeschi, R. G., & Calhoun, L. G. (1996). The Post-traumatic Growth Inventory: Measuring the positive legacy of trauma. *Journal of Traumatic Stress*, 9(3), 455–471

Tedeschi, R. G., & Calhoun, L, G. (2004). Post-traumatic Growth: Conceptual Foundations and Empirical Evidence. *Psychological Inquiry*, 15(1), 1–18

Thoits, P. A. (1994). Stressors and problem-solving: The individual as psychological activist. *Journal of Health and Social Behavior*, Vol 35 (2) June 1994, 143–160

Thompson, J., & Gomez, R. (2014). The Role of Self-Esteem and Self-Efficacy in Moderating the Effect of Workplace Stress on Depression, Anxiety and Stress. *Australasian Journal of Organisational Psychology*, 7, e2

Thompson, K. R., Hochwarter, W. A., & Mathys, N. J. (1997). Stretch targets: What makes them effective? *The Academy of Management Executive*, 11(3), 48–60

Tierney, P., & Farmer, S. M. (2002). Creative self-efficacy: Its potential antecedents and relationship to creative performance. *Academy of Management Journal*, 45(6), 1137–1148

Toor, S.-U.-R., & Ofori, G. (2009). Authenticity and its influence on psychological well-being and contingent self-esteem of leaders in Singapore construction sector. *Construction Management and Economics, 27*(3), 299–313. doi: 10.1080/01446190902729721

Truce, C. (30 May 2017). Knowledge economy in financial services: from curator to conductor. Saxo Bank. www.home.saxo/en-au/campaigns/mpu/wlc/2017/6/knowledge-economy-in-financial-services-from-curator-to-conductor, accessed 12 February 2021

Tsang, E. W. (1997). Organizational learning and the learning organization: a dichotomy between descriptive and prescriptive research. *Human Relations, 50*(1), 73–89

Tuten, T. L., & Neidermeyer, P. E. (2004). Performance, satisfaction and turnover in call centers. *Journal of Business Research, 57*(1), 26–34. doi: 10.1016/S0148-2963(02)00281-3

Videka-Sherman, L., & Lieberman, M. (1985). The effects of self-help and psychotherapy intervention on child loss: The limits of recovery. *American Journal of Orthopsychiatry, 55*(1), 70–82. doi: 10.1111/j.1939-0025.1985.tb03422.x

Wagnild, G. M., & Young, H. M. (1993). Development and psychometric evaluation of the Resilience Scale. *Journal of Nursing Measurement, 1*(2), 165–178

Walumbwa, F. O., & Schaubroeck, J. (2009). Leader Personality Traits and Employee Voice Behavior: Mediating Roles of Ethical Leadership and Work Group Psychological Safety. *Journal of Applied Psychology*, 94(5), 1275–1286. doi: 10.1037/a0015848

Weick, K. E., & Quinn, R. E. (1999). Organizational change and development. *Annual Review of Psychology*, 50, 361–386. doi: 10.1146/annurev.psych.50.1.361

Werner, E. E. (1993). Risk, Resilience, and Recovery – Perspectives from the Kauai Longitudinal-Study. *Development and Psychopathology*, 5(4), 503–515

Wheeler, S. C., Briñol, P., & Hermann, A. D. (2007). Resistance to persuasion as self-regulation: Ego-depletion and its effects on attitude change processes. *Journal of Experimental Social Psychology*, 43(1), 150–156. doi: 10.1016/j.jesp.2006.01.001

Willis, J. (2010). The current impact of neuroscience on teaching and learning. In *Mind, Brain and Education: Neuroscience Implications for the Classroom*, 45–68. Solution Tree Press, Bloomington, IL

Wood, R., & Bandura, A. (1989). Impact of Conceptions of Ability on Self-Regulatory Mechanisms and Complex Decision Making. *Journal of Personality and Social Psychology*, 56(3), 407–415. doi: 10.1037//0022-3514.56.3.407

Wood, R., Bandura, A., & Bailey, T. (1990). Mechanisms governing organizational performance in complex decision-making environments. *Organizational Behavior and Human Decision Processes*, 46(2), 181–201. doi: 10.1016/0749-5978(90)90028-8

Worrall, L., & Cooper, C. (2012). *Quality of Working Life 2012: Managers' Wellbeing, Motivation and Productivity Report*. Chartered Management Institute, www.researchgate.net/publication/290440383, accessed February 2021

Wortman, C.B. (2004). Posttraumatic growth: Progress and problems. *Psychological Inquiry*, 15(1), 1–90

Youssef, C. M., & Luthans, F. (2007). Positive organizational behavior in the workplace – The impact of hope, optimism, and resilience. *Journal of Management*, 33(5), 774–800. doi: 10.1177/0149206307305562

Zautra, A. J., & Reich, J. W. (2010). Resilience: The Meanings, Methods, and Measures of Human Adaptation. In *The Oxford Handbook of Stress, Health, and Coping*, 173. Oxford Library of Psychology, Oxford

Further Resources

For copies of the questionnaires, more information, training or consulting, go to www.drsammather.com.

Acknowledgements

Thank you to all those who have supported, encouraged and inspired me.

To Professor Patricia Riddell and Dr Dorota Bourne, both of whom have supported me through my research and taught me so much.

To my family, my mum and especially my sister Karen and step-mum Julie whom I cajoled into reading each draft chapter. Thank you both for your eye for detail and constructive feedback.

And to my friends, Sean, Tracy, Jo, Grace, Wendy and my oldest friend Gilly, who all believed in me, even when I didn't.

This book was partially funded using GoFundMe. Grateful thanks to those who contributed, especially Sean, Mark, Paula, Steve, Arthur, Sandra, Keren, Tim, Nick, Darren and all those who wanted to remain anonymous. You know who you are. Thank you.

The Author

Dr Sam Mather discovered neuroscience later in life, although she likes to describe it as her 'prime'. After decades developing leaders in international organisations, she was still seeing (and experiencing) poor leadership. What was it that prevented the application of good leadership practice? She was so curious – not only about what made a great leader but *how* – that she returned to university to pursue her PhD in organisational psychology. This journey introduced her to neuroscience, which provided her with the 'how'. In understanding the mechanisms of the brain that control how we feel and behave, she was able to apply science to what her delegates and coachees used to call the 'soft' aspect of leadership: people management. Being an effective leader was no longer pink and fluffy: it was scientific!

Armed with her three years of research, her knowledge of neuroscience, many years of experience in industry and sense of humour, Dr Sam has written this book for leaders who want to improve the performance of their people and ultimately their organisation by starting with themselves.

Dr Sam Mather has gained her experience across four continents, in a range of industries, supporting organisations with their employee development, change management, HR practices, diversity and inclusion, and recruitment. She is also a qualified coach, neuroscience practitioner, NLP practitioner and entertaining speaker. She currently lives in Berkshire in the UK.

Other books written by Dr Sam include *RISE: The science and practice of creating and developing your cognitive resources for resilience and well-being*.

⊕ www.drsammather.com

Milton Keynes UK
Ingram Content Group UK Ltd.
UKHW022155220923
429169UK00009B/60